HOT GUYS AND SHOULDER CRIES

Hot Guys and Shoulder Cries

Felicia Paulozza

Published by Life Rattle Press

Published in 2014 by Life Rattle Press New Publishing Series, a division of Life Rattle Press.

www.liferattle.ca

Library and Archives Canada Cataloguing in Publication

Paulozza, Felicia
    Hot Guys & Shoulder Cries

Issued in Print Only
ISBN 978-1-927023-709

Cover Design by Felicia Paulozza

Printed and Bound by CreateSpace

A Little Thank You...

I would like to take this opportunity to thank everyone who has contributed in helping me with the process of writing this book. I would also like to thank the guys who inspired these stories, if it wasn't for you, well, I wouldn't have had these stories in the first place.

Thank you to Professor Guy Allen for believing in my writing and guiding me through this process. You were one of my toughest critics, but without you I would not be where I am in my writing career. Any students who take your courses are in for a fun and life changing experience.

This book is dedicated to all the people who have believed in me from day one, to you reading this book right now and to all the new writers struggling to write their own book.

Thank you and enjoy,

Felicia xoxo

Contents

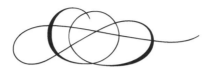

MASH

MASH

"When I went to school, they asked me what I wanted to be when I grew up. I wrote down 'Happy'. They told me I didn't understand the assignment and I told them they didn't understand life."

-John Lennon

ASH is a very popular game that is played to determine the future husbands of my friends and I. With MASH, every week my future husband could change from Dave, to Mike, to Dan, to Chris.

This week MASH says I'm supposed to marry Greg. The only problem is, MASH told Sophia and Chloe that they were supposed to marry Greg too.

Today's my shot to show Greg that I am going to be the best future wife ever. I wore my brand new Le Chateau patched jeans that I bought on the weekend and my bubblegum pink golf shirt. My blonde highlighted hair is pin straight and I slapped on my favorite MAC foundation, bronzer, and black eyeliner to highlight my bright hazel eyes.

No one could look better than me today, except, well, Sophia and Chloe. I have fierce competition.

What am I going to do? To be honest, I think that Greg has a thing for Sophia. My life is over.

Something happened at school today. I think that Greg might like me.

It rained today, and since Greg and I are in the same class, we were able to share all three recesses together.

On lunch recess. Greg, Chloe, Dave, Dan and I gather in a circle.

"Hey guys let's play signal," Dave says. He looks at Chris, "You're my partner."

Chloe and I glare at each other and mentally choose each other as partners.

Greg interrupts our stare conversation, taps me and says, "Hey Felicia, want to be my partner?"

No words utter from my mouth for about ten seconds.

He wants to be my partner.

"Um," I stutter, "Yea sure." I look at Chloe, "Is that okay?"

"Ya Feli," Chloe giggles. "Dan will be my partner."

While Dave deals the cards, Greg and I decide what our signal is. When Greg has signal he winks, and when I have signal I cough. It works because I feel like I am catching a cold, so it's not obvious.

Dave and Chris win 10 rounds of signal. Greg and I only win one round.

I really like Greg and I need to know if he feels the same.

Yesterday, Sophia said Greg was flirting with her at recess. He cracked her back for her.

That's our thing. He always cracks my back.

I told my friend Ashley to ask Greg if he likes me or Chloe or Sophia. Chloe doesn't seem to care who Greg likes. I think she likes Greg, but not a lot. I think she is more into Dan.

"So I asked Greg who he liked when we walked home from school today," Ashley calls my house phone after school to clarify if MASH was right.

Am I going to marry Greg?

"What did he say? Does he like me? Does he have a crush on Sophia? He likes Chloe doesn't he?"

"Well, he told me that he met up with his ex Natasha after school last week." My heart races. "He said he still kind of likes Natasha."

"So that's not that bad. At least he doesn't like Sophia or Chloe. Right?"

"Well, he said he likes Natasha still, but he also likes Sophia. Sorry Feli," Ashley says in a saddened voice.

MASH was wrong.

"It's okay, I don't want to chime in on their relationship. Plus I played MASH again this week twice, you know for a back up. It said that I'm going to marry either Mike or Dave. I hope it's Dave."

MASH also told me when I get married, I will have four kids, drive a SUV and live in a mansion and have a super rich life. I hope the rest comes true.

GRAD

GRAD

"Thank goodness for best friends. For true friends, the ones who love you no matter what."
-Lauren Clark

A bus limo waits outside my house for twenty of my friends and I to board. The same twenty friends that I spend every recess, every day after school, every weekend and every party with.

Adriana, Sophia, Chloe, Isabella and I are all single ladies and decide to go solo at our Grade 8 grad party tonight. Each of us bought a brand new dress got our hair curled and our make-up professionally done.

My dress is bubblegum pink with spaghetti straps and floral beading along the side of my stomach. It's short in the front, with light pink chiffon ruffles that flow down longer in the back. I accessorize with silver jewelry and sliver shoes, topped with a mini silver tiara in my hair.

Mike, one of my best friends, looks mighty fine in his black suit and red dress shirt. The spikes in his hair, sculpted by gel. I've had a major crush on Mike since we met in grade four in my cousin Madison's basement.

A few weeks ago, I went to a bridal shower and the bride brought in a psychic to determine the future of the ladies at the party. The psychic said I am going to fall in love within the next two years. I think that it's Mike. Soon he'll realize that he loves me.

Mike is really into the super skinny girls with no curves. He needs to get over it. I have curves, I'm chesty and I'm not a toothpick but I'm not fat.

After the dinner, we race to the dance floor. The DJ spins all our favorite songs, from 'Hollarback Girl' by Gwen Stefani to 'In da Club' by 50 Cent.

As we soak the dance floor with preteen sweat and allow our body odor to seep into the wooden dance floor, Prinicpal Costa asks the DJ to stop the music.

"Students, can I have you all sit down for a moment please?" Principal Costa stands at the podium that faces the round tables in the hall. Everyone heads back to their tables and listens to what Principal Costa has to say. "I just want to congratulate you all on this great accomplishment and wish you the best of luck in the future."

I feel a tear drip down my cheek.

Uh oh.

I wipe my cheek and under my eye so my eyeliner doesn't smudge.

Principal Costa's Wal-Mart bought glasses begin to fog up. "I have had the greatest opportunity to watch you all progress into wonderful teens. You are going to have an amazing experience in high school."

Tears shower my face. I glance around the room and see my friends crying, the teachers crying and the chaperon moms crying. I look ahead. Mike grasps my attention. He shakes his head and pouts, then smiles. I smile and wipe the tears from under my eyes and all over my cheeks.

"I cannot wait to see what you kids accomplish. Please come back and visit. Enjoy the rest of your night." We applaud and music resumes to 'Graduation' by Vitamin C.

The instrumental of the song begins to play as Mike walks toward me. My friends and I sit in a circle and cry. "What's wrong Feli?" He asks.

"Nothing," I weep.

"Feli," Mike tilts his head to the side and stares me in the eyes. Tears continue to pour down my face.

Mike pulls me up from my chair and hugs me, "can you tell me why you're crying?"

"Because," I wipe my nose with the overused tissue in my hand. "What if we don't all stay friends in high school? I love you guys." I rest my head on Mike's shoulder and sob. Mike hugs me and rubs my back.

The chorus of the song plays, "Oh great," I sigh. I wipe my eyes and sniff the snot that drips from my nose. "This is really going to help."

Mike guides me to the dance floor. He places my hands around his neck, wraps his hands around my waist and we dance to the slow beat of the song.

"As we go on, we remember, all the times we've, had together. " I weep and Mike holds me closer and sings along with the track playing, "and as our lives change, from whatever, we will still be, friends forever." I smile, and the teardrops dry on my face.

The song ends, I pull away from Mike and look at him with my puffy hazel eyes that now faded to a shade of green.

"Thank you. I needed that." I hug him.

"Anything for my BFFL." Mike tucks my hair behind my ear and wipes the remaining tears off. "Feli, we're going to be friends in high school and after high school, I promise."

I sigh, and wipe any leftover tears from underneath my eyes. "Okay, fine I believe you." Mike looks at me, and we giggle. "You're the best Mike."

CAF
BOY

CAF BOY

"You'll always miss 100% of the shots you don't take."
-Wayne Gretzky

Three months into grade 9, Chloe and I seem to have our lunch routine down pact. From weeks one to three, we bring our own lunch and completely avoid the cafeteria, until week four.

On week four, I grab Chloe's hand and pull her through the sardine-squished crowd. We wait in the massive line up of students who fight to get into the two doors that separate them from the cafeteria where everyone eats and the cafeteria (aka the caf) where they buy their food.

On week four, my hair is straightened everyday. On week four, I wear my kilt. After I leave my house I roll up my kilt twice, about four inches shorter than it's required length.

On week four Caf Boy leans back against the side of the doorway, his long pale arm stretches across with his hand pressed against it, and his lanky leg blocks the bottom of the doorway with his black dress shoe squished against the other side.

I spotted Caf Boy two months ago. The only communication we've had, is when Caf Boy turns his perfectly shaved head to look down at me and says "Okay, you can go now."

As Christmas break approaches, 'The Big Event' is soon to come. The event consists of a handful of students who perform their talents in front of a gym filled of relieved teachers who don't have to teach, and grateful students who don't have to pretend to learn.

Some say it's fun, others say it's lame, and don't bother to go to school at all, my friends included. They've never seen the event but already labeled it as 'boring'. I'm going to check it out.

The whole ensemble reminds me a lot of the Christmas concert on Mean Girls. The more popular students are cheered on by their peers, and the others are applauded by faculty.

People sing, some are actually decent. Others need to stick to being a student and continue working their part-time job at McDonald's. A few people showed off their years of dance their parents forced them through. All routines include a bit of Ballet, Jazz, Hip-Hop, and Acro.

The final act is called on stage.

"Okay ladies and gents," the principal announces. "Let's give it up for the B-Town Villagers!." The crowd cheers.

The gym is black, and the song "Call on Me" by Eric Prydz shouts through the speakers. Six spotlights gleam on six guys, dressed in black champion tear away pants and a white tank top. As the song hits the chorus, the six guys dance in sync, like a promiscuous version of the Backstreet Boys.

Air humping, butt shaking, and girls screaming, the guys rip off their black tear away pants and floss them between their crotches.

Oh, my, god! That's the guy from the caf!

I jump up from the cold gym floor and stare as The B-town Villagers continue to thrust the air.

Their performance finishes, and the crowd screams for an encore. Due to the semi inappropriate dance, the principal doesn't allow it. The B-Town Villagers is crowned with the first prize.

I call Chloe to tell her about the amazing event that she and the rest of the girls missed out on.

"Feli," Chloe says, "I know who Caf Boy is."

"You do? How the hell do you know him, and who is he?

Well I knew he looked familiar, so I searched through our elementary school yearbook from grade 6 and I found him. He was in grade eight and his name is Nick. Nick Anderson."

"Are you sure? Because I used to put hearts all the hot grade 8's, who I categorized as 'marriage material'. I don't remember seeing Caf Boy. I mean Nick."

"Yes," Chloe assured me. "He used to be fat."

That explains it.

"No way! Well now I know his name. This is progress! Now, I need to figure out how to talk to him."

Christmas break is over. My mission to talk to Nick resumes. Not many people know about my crush. Only my close friends. Maybe if I told more people I would find a way to talk to him.

I tell my friend Pina, from English class, about Caf Boy. She tells me that she knows him and that she has him as a friend on TDotmeetup.com. It is a site where you can talk to people who you find attractive, instead of having courage and doing it face-to-face.

Plan A is set in motion. After school, I create an account on TDotmeetup.com. I find Pina, add her as a friend and search her friends and find Nick. I wait five minutes and add Nick.

Friend request accepted.

"Hey Hun looking good," I press enter and the message is sent to Nick.

Will he even reply? Does he even know who I am? Does he even think I am pretty or hot?

I pace my room for fifteen minutes and stare at Nick's profile picture.

His picture gives him no justice. It's super dark and you can barely see his stern face starring into -what I assume is -the web-cam above the computer screen.

A message pops up onto my screen from the TDotmeetup.com website. The message is from Nick.

"Hey Hun, thanks you to. How was your day?"

My hands tremble and my stomach growls.

I'm not even hungry. Oh my God, he wants to know how my day was.

After three days of back and forth small talk, Nick suggests we bring our conversation over to MSN.

This is a big step in our cyber relationship.

We exchange emails, so we can instantly message each other whenever we want! Nick sends me his soccer inspired email over the chat in TDotmeetup.com.

I add milan_4life79@hotmail.com to my MSN, and Nick accepts my request from xoxpurplechickitaxox@hotmail.com.

I need to get a new email. This is from like grade six.

Nick and I talk a lot. From talking about our days, to the friends we hang out with, to the elementary school we went to and whatever our weekend plans were.

I am supposed to go to my dad's this weekend and I tell Nick how I really don't want to go.

Over the weekend, I am on MSN every hour. Even when I am not at my laptop my status is always set to 'Online', just in case Nick messages me.

On Friday night, Nick messages me. On Saturday, I message Nick. And on Sunday, Nick messages me and I vent to him about my weekend at my dad's house.

It became a bi-weekly event for me to vent to Nick about my weekend at my dad's house. On the other weekends I gloat about how much fun I had with my friends.

Once every season, an all ages Waybacks Event is held at a club about twenty minutes away from Bolton.

Sin City, a standalone building in it's own plaza, just off the 400 in Vaughan, Ontario. It used to be called Palazzo.

Wayback events consist of every old school Euro song you can think of, mixed with a bunch of horny, sweaty teenagers grinding and jumping around with strangers and friends.

My first Waybacks Event, and all I can think about is how hot I have to look because Nick is going to be there tonight. Tonight's mission, dance with Nick.

Sophia, Adriana, Isabella, Chloe and I walk into the room of Euro blasting sound and head to the dance floor. Adriana and Isabella have to use the bathroom. Chloe joins them. Sophia and I head to the crowded dance floor. We find an empty space and start jamming to Cascada's song 'Miracle'.

As Sophia and I sing the lyrics to each other, her eyes brighten up and she points behind me. "Look," she mouths.

I turn my head and I see Nick. "Oh my god," I fan myself.

"I'm in love. Ahh!!"

Sophia and I continue to dance, and my favorite song, "I Dream" by Waldo's People plays. I bust out my best moves.

"I Dream of the love is all around you, I dream of that I can stay forever with you now..." Sophia and I pull out our invisible glow-sticks.

We move closer toward Nick and his friends. "Golddigger" by Kanye West ft. Jamie Fox plays.

Nick's friend Gianfranco grabs Sophia from behind. They grind. Sophia's eyebrows arch up and down, and then someone pulls me backwards into -what I assume is- a guy's body. Long, pale, lanky arms wrap around my body.

Sophia smiles at me as if it is Nick who just grabbed me. I turn my head. Nick smiles, and I blush. I turn my head back around and continue grinding with Nick.

Nick. Nick Anderson is actually grinding with me.

As I bubble my butt into his crotch, the song plays, "Get down girl go ahead get down, get down go ahead get down..." We get lower and lower to the ground and slowly grind back up again.

My legs are killing. Suck it up Felicia and keep bubbling that ass into his crotch.

After a few more songs, Nick and I take a little break. Nick whispers into my ear "I'll be back" and goes to join his friends. I nod back. Sophia and I search for Adriana, Isabella and Chloe. We find them across the room, standing in a secluded area chatting with some of our guy friends.

Nick is no longer in sight. I jump up and down and tell the girls about the magical dance Nick and I shared. The girls laugh.

"I saw you from here." Adriana says, "and I can tell you were loving it."

My face heats up. "What do you mean you can tell I was loving it? What did I look like?"

"You had a perma-smile on your face, and he was so into it. He was like canoodling you as you guys were grinding," Adriana explains, and I sigh into a daze.

"We're in love," I rest my hand on my heart. I look across the club and see Nick. He winks at me. I can't wink. I smile back and Nick walks closer and closer toward me.

Nick grabs me and leads me back onto the dance floor. Round two.

The Euro songs sound muffled and my surroundings are blurred. I see Nick's arms wrapped around my body, and when he spun me around his flawless face with his dark brown eyes starring into my hazel eyes. I feel like I am living the dream.

It's not a dream. It's not a dream because this perfect moment is ruined with a vibration in my bra. It's 12:15AM, dance time is over, like Cinderella at the ball. The vibration means my mom is calling and I have to leave the club. My horse and carriage is waiting for me outside, aka my mom in her SUV.

I grab my phone from my bra. Confirmed. My mom is outside. I have to go. I turn to Nick and show him my phone flashing as my mom calls. "I have to go," my eyes pout.

Nick's smile turns into a semi-frown. "Bye, nice seeing you." Nick kisses me on the cheek I close my eyes and sigh.

"Bye," I wave and rush out the club.

Two days later.

Nick and I chat for over five hours via MSN. I stare at the computer screen anticipating Nick's reply to everything I say.

Over the hours and hours of talking, Nick opens up to me more and more. Turns out we have a lot in common.

This is Caf Boy. I dreamed of us falling in love, but I never actually thought my dreams would ever come true.

What the fuck, its midnight who the hell is calling me? My cell phone's disco ring tone plays through the speaker.

I look at the little square screen on the front of my phone and I see a random number that consists of 6's and 8's.

"Um, hello?" I answer my phone and pace my room.

"Hey, its Nick," He replies. "What's up?"

I feel as if my heart drops down to my toes, "Nothing, just getting ready for bed, you?"

"Not much. I'm in bed now and I didn't feel like typing anymore. Your number was in your MSN name so I decided to call you" Nick explains. "I hope that's okay?"

"Oh my gosh, ya it's fine," I chuckle.

Nick and I talk until 2:30AM.

Nick's parents are divorced, his relationship with his dad isn't the best and his mom is with a mangia cake man.

My relationship with my dad is on the rocks. My parents are divorced. My mom is remarried to a mangia cake man.

A mangia cake is a term Italians refer to Canadian/Irish/ Scottish people as. Nick's mom is expecting a baby this summer. My mom had a baby boy a two years ago.

Nick vents to me about his relationship with his dad. Nick said that he had to escape from it. Nick did the right thing to get out of that negative environment. I don't have the courage that Nick had to step out of that.

I explain to Nick that my relationship with my dad needs to change. He thinks every step I take and everything that comes out of my mouth is my mom 'conditioning' me to say these things.

I think we are at about World War 25 when it comes to negotiating any weekend switches, when there is a party or some event I want to go to with my friends. It's my mom who wants me to switch, of course.

Why would I ever want to hang out with my friends on the weekends? Why would I ever want to go to parties on the weekend? Who doesn't want to spend every other weekend sitting at home, doing chores and watching movies while their friends are all out together.

"It's all me," I explain to Nick, "but my dad just doesn't get it."

I just want to be a normal teen and go to the parties with my friends. I don't want to miss out on anything.

"I'm sorry, I keep going on about it. I don't want to bore you."

"Feli-"

I love that he calls me Feli.

"If I didn't want to know I wouldn't have called you and asked you about it," Nick re-assures me.

He's perfect.

In grade 7, just after his parents separated, Nick stood up to his father. He wants me to stand up for myself, but I don't have the courage he did.

Not only do I hear grief when I want to switch weekends, depending on his mood, if I want to watch TV, I need to make sure all the chores are done. I have to cook, clean and do the laundry while he has meetings with his friend, Mary Jane. If I don't set the table right, I have to re-do it. If I don't load the dishwasher properly, I have to re-load it.

"Feli, when I told my dad where to go it was the best thing I ever did." Nick says. "I felt so much happier. My mom raised me not my dad."

"I know, I know. When the time is right I will do it. I think it might be soon though."

"When you're ready you will know. I know we don't know each other that well and for long, but I haven't shared this much with anyone, ever. My friends don't even know as much as I just shared. Just please don't say anything," he begs.

"I feel the same. None of my friends really get what I go through. I know a few of them see it, but they have never lived it. And, no don't worry I won't say anything, it's not my business to."

"Holy, it's 2:30am, I'm pooped." Nick yawns into the speaker and I stare at the time on the cable box above my TV. "I'll see you at school tomorrow. Goodnight Feli".

"Goodnight," I say, and press end.

Two hours and thirty-three minutes. Nick and I were on the phone for two hours and thirty-three minutes.

I flop on my bed, sigh and hold my phone to my chest.

A few months have passed and 'Mission: Make Nick my Boyfriend' has hit a plateau. Nick and I have gathered both of our groups of friends into one big one. We hang out almost every single weekend.

Everyday, Nick and I talk, at school, through text, on the phone and on MSN. I don't know if he likes me or just sees me as a good friend. Nick's friend Gianfranco always teases me and says that I like Nick. I always deny it and every time I slip out an innocent laugh that indicates Gianfranco is right. My friends think he likes me, but I'm still not convinced.

My hands tremble over the keyboard, my stomach grumbles, "Hey loser whats-up." I message Nick on MSN.

Time to tell Nick the truth. I don't know how he is going to respond, but I know that I cant handle being his friend anymore. I know he knows that we're not 'just friends', but I don't know if he really knows it.

My screen reads, Nick is writing a message, "Hey, not much

just got home from school, you?"

I take a deep breath, "Not much," I press enter.

"Okay so basically, everyone already knows, but I just thought I would get it out in the open."

Enter.

Nick is writing a message. Nick stops writing a message.

"Nick I kind of sort of like you."

I take another deep breath. Butterflies invade my stomach.

Nick is writing a message, and the butterflies in my stomach throw a party.

"Feli, you're a really nice girl," and my heart begins to shatter into small pieces.

Time to bring out the ice cream.

"I just don't know what I want yet. I really like you as a friend and I hope we can stay friends."

"Yea sure no problem just thought I would let you know. Don't worry nothing will change".

Three days later. Nick messages me on MSN.

"Hey Feli."

"Hey, what's up?"

"Well, I've been thinking." I read, and my face freezes.

"After you told me you liked me, every time I saw you I kept thinking. I kept thinking, I don't want to be just your friend Feli." Nick continues.

I gulp the puddle of drool that floods my mouth.

"Really?" I ask, and then copy and paste the conversation to Adriana.

"I like you Feli. I really like you. I feel so different with you. I feel like you get me and I can tell you anything. I haven't ever felt this way about anyone."

I sit in my computer chair and stare at the screen. I read the message to myself over and over again.

I really like you. He likes me. He really likes me. We're in love.

I send Nick a big happy face, "Phew, I'm so glad to hear you say that."

"Woohoo!" I shout in my room, jump out of my chair and begin dancing in front of my mirror.

THE
SWITCH

THE SWITCH

"Maybe there's something you're afraid to say, or someone you're afraid to love, or somewhere you're afraid to go. It's gonna hurt. It's gonna hurt because it matters."

-John Green

"Feli, are you coming Saturday?" Nick asks. "I really want you to come."

Nick and I have been 'dealing' – the high school version of dating but not exclusive - for only a couple of months now. He turns 17 years old next Tuesday, and on Friday his friend Gianfranco is throwing him a big bash at his house. His house is located in the middle of nowhere on some back road in Bolton. He has a huge backyard with countless acres of land.

I want to go, but it's my Dad's weekend. This would be my first high school party. All the grade 11's and 12's will be there, and of course only my crew of grade 9 girls.

"Ugh, I don't know, I want to." I tug on my duvet to cover my bed, "I am going to see what my Dad says, if he'll switch" I throw my pillows on each side and leap onto my freshly made bed.

"I don't know why you're so scared to tell him. Feli, you don't deserve this shit." Nick flops on my bed beside me, powers on my TV, and tunes to our favorite show, 'Deal or No Deal'.

"I know. I'm not like you though. I'm too scared. But I don't want to miss your birthday. This is not fair man." I rest my head on Nick's chest and he wraps his arms around me and holds me closer to him.

Three shows later, my cellphone vibrates on my bed. I look down at the screen and see my dad's number flashing along to the ring tone.

"Hi dad," I hop off my bed and pace my room.

"Hi hunny, what are you doing? I am just getting ready for bed."

"Nothing. Me too." I say, "So, Dad, there is this party this weekend and um, well all the girls are going and I really want to go. I am not going to come this weekend. We'll just switch and I'll come visit you for two weekends in a row after this weekend."

I take a deep breath. My palms sweat. My heart thumps out of my chest.

"You know what Felicia," the tone of my dad's voice heightens, "I am sick and tired of this switching weekends bullshit."

"What do you mean dad? I never ask you. Do you know how many parties I've missed?"

"What? Did your mother say she's going to bring you shopping for a new outfit if you go to this party?" I roll my eyes and look at Nick.

"What's he saying?" Nick mouths to me as my father continues to rant.

"Um, NO! I just want to go, like all my friends are going."

I crawl onto my bed and lay down beside Nick. Nick presses his ear against the other side of my phone to hear the conversation. I stare at the wall and the ceiling and the door and the muted TV. My dad continues to rant about how my mother talked me into this.

"I had plans this weekend for us Felicia."

He always 'has plans' for us. His plans mean cleaning the house, or going to Costco and walking down every single aisle twice, or visiting my grandparents and my cousins. We can do that any weekend.

"You always have plans for us dad. I am in high school now. I want to go out with my friends. The plans can hold off for next weekend. Common Dad, please I really want to go!" I whine.

Friday.

If I go home on my bus from school I know my dad is going to be waiting for me outside my stop. Instead, I hop on my friend Sophia's bus with her, and my mom waits for us outside Sophia's bus stop.

My phone vibrates in my bra. I pull it out and look at the screen. I turn to my mom. "It's my dad. I don't want to go."

"Answer it. Tell him you don't want to go then."

"Hello" I answer my phone.

"Hunny, where are you?" My dad asks.

"Dad please, I am not coming tonight. I am going to my friend's party. I'll come tomorrow or we'll switch weekends and I will make it a double weekend."

"Hunny, please. Why are you doing this? I told you that I'm not switching weekends. I had plans for us." He begs.

"Dad, it's always the same thing. I'm older now and I want to hang out with my friends. I am sorry but you're not listening to what I have to say."

"Come on hunny."

I hold the phone to my chest and whisper to my mom. "He isn't going to leave."

My mom looks into the rearview mirror at Sophia, "I am sorry you have to witness this, but we have no other choice and we don't know what is going to happen. It's better that you're here with us."

"Its okay," Sophia sits up straight, behind the driver's seat. She stares outside the window at the cars driving past us toward her subdivision.

I put the phone back to my ear, "Dad meet us at the police station down the hill."

"What?! Felicia please hunny can we just solve this without the cops?"

I look into my reflection in the visor mirror. Blood peeps through my cheeks. My eyes round and widen. I look down at the sweat that drips from the palm of my hand onto the black leather seat. I wipe my hands on my black dress pants. My temples pulse. My legs shake.

"Dad, please just meet us there."

Two minutes driving down Highway 50, we arrive at the Ontario Provincial Police station, downtown Bolton. My mom, Sophia and I get out of the car and walk into the station.

A tall, pale, shaved head police officer dressed in the classic black attire, approaches us at the front desk. "Hello ladies, how can I help you today?"

"We need some advice," my mom says. "Her father is on the way." My mom points at me. "She doesn't want to go to her father's house this weekend, and he refuses to switch weekends."

"Well-" the officer responds. My dad swings the door open and storms into the station.

"Guys please don't do this," my Dad begs.

"Sir, I am going to ask your daughter to tell me the story

with both you and your ex-wife present."

My hands sweat again. The sweat drips from the palm of my hand onto the white tiled floor.

"So basically," I look down at the dirty white floor. "Whenever I want to switch weekends, my dad gets pissed." I turn to my dad, "I'm in high school dad, there are going to be parties and I am going to want to go to them."

"I know hunny but you can't go to all of them. What about our weekends?"

"Sir," The officer approaches my dad, "She has had the choice since she was thirteen, to participate in the custody agreement to visit either you or your ex wife."

As the officer continues to explain, I move my body closer so I can hear everything clearly. "As of now she is saying she wants to stay. I am sorry sir but there is nothing you can do about it," the officer adds.

A tear drops down my dad's cheek. My eyes begin to water. *Be strong.*

I wipe the tears from under my eyes.

You have come this far. You know what happens when the tears aren't there. Nothing is going to change.

My cellphone constantly vibrates in my bra. It's a long vibration, which means someone is calling me.

It's probably Nick wondering if I'm going tonight.

"Okay well I guess it is what it is," my dad shrugs his shoulders and kisses my forehead. "Bye hunny, I'll call you later."

He storms out the police station, gets into his black pick-up truck, and his wheels screech as he zooms off.

My phone vibrates. "It's Nick again," I look to my mom.

"Hey, I'm coming now." I answer.

"Feli, can you please hurry, I want you to come it's already 10:30." Nick begs.

"Yes, Nick I am coming now. I'll be there soon."

"Okay text me when you are down the street."

I arrive to the party, and Nick waits at the end of the rocky driveway. His face brightens as my mom drives up next to him. I get out of the car, run and hug Nick.

"Hi Patricia, thanks for bringing her," Nick says.

"Hey Nick, no problem." She turns to me, "Felicia, I'll be here around 12:30 to pick you up. Nick are you coming too?"

"Alright, how about one? " I smirk.

"Yea, if that's okay," Nick adds.

"Fine, bye" my mom smiles and drives off.

I slowly walk up the driveway toward the backyard of blaring music and drunk teens.

"How did it go with your dad?" Nick grabs my hand and pulls me toward him.

"The officer said I didn't have to go anymore if I didn't want to. My dad seemed pissed but honestly, I am done. I felt bad for my dad, but whatever I am better off now."

"Feli, you'll be okay."

Nick gently pulls me toward his chest, lifts up my chin and looks into my watering eyes. Nick wipes the tears that drip down my cheek and kisses me softly. He hugs close and snug, right against his rapidly beating heart. Warmth surrounds my body, as I sigh in relief.

"Can we just stay here until my mom comes?" I mumble.

Nick giggles, and grabs my hand linking our hands together, as we walk toward the backyard.

"Come on, let's go. The girls are waiting for you."

FIRST
BUT
NEVER
LAST

FIRST BUT NEVER LAST

"If she's amazing, she won't be easy. If she's easy, she won't be amazing. If she is worth it, you wont give up. If you give up, you're not worthy. Truth is, everybody is going to hurt you. You just gotta find the ones worth suffering for."
-Bob Marley

My heart hammers in my chest. My eyes swell. Tears shower my clothes and my pillow and my sheets. Snot drips down my nose.

Nick and I broke up a week ago. After two years. Two years of drama. Two years of older girls cussing at me because Nick and I were an item. Two years of me ditching my friends to hang out with Nick. Two years of my life gone.

I lay in my bed and look through my Nick box. A box of memories of our relationship.

I pull out cue cards with messages from Nick written on them.

I pull out dried up roses from my sweet sixteen.

I pull out a picture of Nick and I at his prom.

I pull out the pink bear that Nick bought me for Valentines Day.

"Five...four...three...two...one...Happy New Year!" The fireworks burst on the TV as Nick and I kiss. It's our first New Year's Eve together.

I text my mom to pick us up and bring us to my house. Our friends are boring. All they want to do is play cards. Nick and I planned on getting drunk tonight.

My mom pick us up and drops us off at my house, then heads back to the neighbors' house - where she was before.

Nick and I lie side-by-side on the leather couch in my living room and watch FRIENDS. Nick lies behind me and cuddles me.

"Just sleep here," I whisper.

"I wish Feli. Our mom's would kill us." Nick lives a two-minute drive from my house.

I turn to face Nick. My heart races as our legs lock together. Nick wraps his arms around me and holds me closer towards him. He kisses me. I kiss him back. I feel a vibration in my crotch area. My phone begins ringing.

"Ugh, it's Michelle" I say to Nick.

"Hello?"

"Feli," my cousin screams through the phone. Loud music plays in the background. She is at a nightclub with friends.

"Yea, Michelle what's wrong?" She calls me crying every time she is drunk.

Michelle attempts to break through her tears and tell me why she is crying. I hold the phone away from my ear as Nick's mom calls his phone because she is waiting outside to pick him up.

"Yea, oh my God?" I say to Michelle. I still don't know what she is saying. "Okay Michelle hold on a second."

I follow Nick to my front door as he slips his shoes on. "I love you," he mouths and kisses me.

I pause.

Did I just see that right?

I put my phone on my ledge in front of the door. "Wait," I call to Nick. "What?"

Nick walks toward me and grabs my hands. I look up at him and pout my eyes. He looks down at me, "I love you Feli."

"I love you too," I sigh and we make-out for a few minutes as his mom continues to wait and Michelle continues to ramble.

"Okay, Feli" Nick smiles, "I have to go. My mom's waiting." He walks outside my front door and turns around to wave.

"Bye, I love you," he says.

I wave back and blow Nick a kiss, "Love you too." I pick up the phone off my ledge and Michelle is still talking. "You're going to be fine. Just go home and get some sleep. Call me tomorrow."

"Okay," Michelle catches her breath from her tears and hangs up the phone.

Nick texts me before bed, "Feli, what I said tonight, I meant. You're an amazing girl and I am the luckiest guy. I haven't felt this way about anyone in my life. I love you so much."

This weekend is very special. My sixteenth birthday is on Saturday. I rented a bus limo to take twenty of my closest friends and I downtown for dinner.

Nick can't come. We've been arguing about it all week. He is the only one I really want there. He can't come because he just got a new job at a grocery store in town and no one can take his shift.

Saturday.

Nick comes by my house before his shift. "Hey Feli," Nick kisses my cheek.

"Hi," I stare at myself in my full-length mirror in my room as I straighten my hair and get ready for tonight. "I just don't understand how no one can take your shift. Don't they know it's your girlfriend's birthday?"

"Feli, I know. I am sorry. You're being difficult. I told you I would pick you up once the limo drops you guys off after dinner. Can you just open your gift?" Nick hands me a big pink and black birthday bag, stuffed with white tissue.

I open the gift. I pull out a pair of shorts, a pair of pants, three t-shirts and a sweater. "Oh my God, Nick you spoiled me. You didn't have to buy all this." I hug Nick and kiss him. "You know I just want you there, that's why I'm pissed."

"I know Feli. I really want to come, but I promise I will be waiting there for you when you get back and I have another surprise for you."

I have a love/hate relationship with surprises. I always want to know what is going on, but I love when people manage to surprise me. It's hard to surprise me. I was originally going to have a big party at a hall with all my friends, but then I found out that my mom and Nick were trying to surprise me. So, we decided to totally scrap the idea.

"Fine," a half-smile cracks through the frown on my face.

A few hours later.

I'm surrounded my by friends at Jack Astor's restaurant downtown Toronto, but I keep checking my phone for text messages or any calls from Nick.

"What?" I yell at my phone screen.

Nick asked me if he can go to his friend Amanda's party

while he waits for me to come home. I call Nick.

"Hey," he answers. I can hear his step-dad in talking on the phone in the background.

"Where are you?" I demand an answer.

"On my way home from work Feli. Why are you so mad?"

"Because. Like you know I want you here, but yet you ask if you can go to Amanda's party. Like, are you okay?"

"Okay, fine. I won't go Feli. I am sorry. I love you. Call me when you are on your way home. Have fun."

I hang up the phone. "I have to pee," I turn to Sophia, cuing that she is to come with me to the bathroom.

We walk down the steep stairs toward the bathroom.

"Are you okay?" She asks.

"I am just pissed. I don't know where he gets the guts to ask me if he can go to Amanda's birthday?"

Sophia consoles me. "Don't worry Feli. You'll see him soon. We're almost done dinner.. We just need to sing Happy Birthday and then we can go."

I touch up my lip-gloss in the mirror and fluff up my hair. "Do I look okay?" I turn to Sophia.

"Yea, you look hot."

We walk up the stairs, back to the party and sit down at the table. The waitress brings out a big, white birthday cake and my friends begin to sing Happy Birthday.

I squeeze my eyes shut, think, make a wish and blow out the

candles. The waitress cuts the cake and distributes it around the table.

I dig my fork into my slice and Sophia taps me, "Feli, don't you know that guy?" Sophia points to a tall guy with a shaved head who walks toward our table.

"Who?" I cover my mouth full of cake, I look up, and see Nick. I blink my eyes three times, and then rub them to ensure I am not dreaming. Nick holds a bouquet of three white roses. Tears drip down my red face. "I honestly hate you." A smile engraves my mouth.

"I told you I had a surprise," Nick chuckles, hands me the flowers with a card, and gives me a peck on the forehead.

I look around at my friends and they all stare and smile, "You guys all knew?" They nod and laugh. "I hate you guys." I chuckle and I smell the fresh bouquet of roses.

I weep as I snuggle the pink and white teddy bear that Nick bought me. I check my phone to see if Nick replied to any of my messages begging for him back.

No messages.

Nick has been ignoring me for the past two weeks. I thought it was just another normal fight that we have about once every couple months, but I was wrong.

Nick called me the other day and told me that he didn't want to be with me anymore.

I wipe my tears, get up from my bed and wash up. I gather Nick's belongings and pack them in a bag to bring to his house.

I walk toward Nick's house to pick up my stuff and give him back his sweater and a few movies he left here.

I walk across the street toward his house.

Nick drives by.

He stares at me.

He doesn't stop.

BLACK VALENTINE

BLACK VALENTINE

"I don't mind making jokes, but I don't want to look like one."
-Marylin Monroe

I scan the Metro Toronto Convention Center, packed with souped-up Hondas, old school Ferraris and the newest models of Mercedes. Crowds of men drool all around them.

Christian, a guy I have been 'dating' for a couple of months invited me here the other night after he bought me a dozen red roses and took me out to a steak dinner at The Keg. After dinner we went to the movies with my friends.

Best Valentines Day ever.

Why do people care so much about engines and exhaust? How do they know what year and model a car is? Don't they have other things to do? I do admit these old cars are cute. I think I want a pink one. That would be adorable in the summer. My hair blowing in the wind with my sunglasses on and blasting some music. Maybe I should learn about the cars.

My phone vibrates at the bottom of my purse. I search for my phone before it goes to voice mail. Jordan? What does he want?

"Hello?"

"Feli, what's your boyfriend's last name?" My friend Mark Jordan asks in a panic.

"Palleschi. Why?"

"Okay, thanks bye." Call Ended.

I call Jordan back. No ring tone. Straight to voice mail. I call Adriana. Adriana is dating Jordan's best friend, Frank, and I am certain she knows what the deal is.

"Adriana, what the hell is going on? Why is Jordan asking me Christian's last name?"

"Okay Feli," Adriana takes a deep breath, "are you alone?"

I walk away from Christian and his crowd of friends. "Yes. Now what is it?"

"Okay, Feli you know I am telling you this because I love you. I wouldn't lie to you." Adriana explains and takes another deep breath. "Christian, he um, he has a girlfriend."

My body freezes. My mind is blank. "What do you mean he has a girlfriend?" I look around the crowded room of people and I see Christian analyzing me with concern. He looks down at his phone and puts it in his pocket.

"You know Alana?" Adriana asks.

That bitch. I hate Alana. She always writes on Christian's Facebook wall. Christian and Alana met through their cousins, who are best friends.

"Christian and Alana have been dating for like six months. Jordan knows him because he went on a double date with Christian, Alana and one of her friends." Adriana explains.

My jaw drops. I cover my mouth. Tears of anger and hurt leak down my face. I wipe my tears. Christian cannot know that I know.

"Oh my God, Adriana what am I going to do?" I whisper.

"You can't say anything now Feli. Wait until you guys go home today."

"Okay, okay. Oh my God, I have to go. He's coming." I rush Adriana off the phone.

Christian rushes toward me. "Everything okay?" He rubs my back.

"Yea, I'm fine." I smile and walk along with Christian and his friends.

Time passes slowly. My stomach hurts. My heart hurts. My head hurts. Everything hurts. I can't take it anymore.

I storm toward Christian and rapidly tap him on the shoulder until he turns around to face me. "What's up?" He asks.

"What's up?" I flip my hair, "You and me," I point my finger to him and then to me, "we need to talk." My face is red with rage.

Christian's face turns red out of embarrassment. "Okay, what's wrong?"

"Where is your girlfriend?" I stand with my arms crossed and wait for a response.

"What?" Christian's face freezes and his eyes widen.

"Where the fuck is your girlfriend? You know, Alana? Where the fuck is she?" I poke Christian's shoulder and push him away from me.

"What do you mean? She's not my girlfriend." Christian pleads. "I swear we're just friends."

"Just friends?" My voice raises as I throw my hands in the air. "Then why did you go on a double date with Jordan and her friend? Huh? That's how you knew the kind of car he drove! I can't believe I didn't see it."

A few weeks ago while my parents were on vacation Jordan came by my house and when I told Christian he made a comment about the color of the car he drove. I asked him how he knew and he claimed that he saw it at the local coffee shop. I believed him because I figured his cousin knew Jordan so she probably said something.

I laugh. "Did you think I wouldn't find out? That's why I had to beg you to go to the movies with my friends. You thought he was going to be there. You thought you were going to get caught." I storm away from Christian.

"Felicia. Please. I'm sorry." Christian's friends begin to surround us. They all know. I am the only one who didn't know.

Alana calls Christian's phone constantly. He continues to ignore it. A random number calls my phone.

"Hello?" I answer.

"Felicia," a girl on the other line calls me in tears, "it's Alana."

"Are you kidding me? You're actually calling me right now? What do you need Alana?"

"Jordan just called me, he told me everything," Alana sobs so much she can barely speak. "I was going to have sex with him."

"First off, Alana, if you get back with him you're an idiot. I can't talk to you right now. I have to go." I hang up the phone with Alana, search for a secluded area, plant myself on the floor and sob.

How can I be so stupid? How can I not see this? How come the only guy that would get my mind off Nick does this to me?

"Felicia."

Dammit, he found me.

"Just go home with my cousin and we'll talk about this later." I wipe the tears from my eyes and stand up.

"What?" I shout. I point to Christian "You, want me," I point to myself, "to go home with your cousin?" I point to Christian's cousin Jessica who watches us argue. "No frickin way. This is how it's going to go," I explain. "You are going to drive my ass home and we are going to talk about this. You think you can get away with this?"

"No, no" Christian stutters, "fine you can, come home with me."

The subway creeks through the tunnels as a woman announces the next subway stop. "St. Christian station, arriving at St. Christian station."

"Pfft," I comment and glare at Christian. Christian looks down at the floor in shame.

The subway arrives at our stop, "Yorkdale station, arriving at Yorkdale station." The woman announces.

Christian and I step off the subway and get into his friend David's car. David drives Christian and I to his house. The car ride is silent.

"Felicia," Christian utters.

"Do not talk to me right now!" I interrupt.

Twenty minutes later, we arrive at Christian's house and I rush into his truck. Christian walks toward his truck in slow motion with his head starring at the asphalt driveway. He gets into his car, shuts the door and stares outside the window.

"But seriously Christian, did you actually think you were going to get away with this?" I ask. Christian starts his car, backs up out of his driveway, and begins to drive me home.

"I don't know, no," he mumbles.

"Like seriously, Alana and I go to the same damn school!"

"I know," is the only response Christian has as I continue to bitch at him.

Three continuous hours of arguing Christian calls Alana to break up with her. "I just cant' be with you," he says as she begs for him on the other end of the phone.

I sit in Christian's lap, "well I don't know if I can still trust you. I need to think." I peck Christian on the lips, hop out of his truck and walk into my house.

I slam my locker door shut and I see Alana. She stands in front of me holding her textbooks and smilies.

"What do you want Alana?" I turn my head and walk down the hall toward my classroom.

"Have you spoken to Christian?" She chases after me.

"No, why?"

"Well, I did, I think we are going to work on things," she says in excitement.

I stop in the middle of the hallway, turn to face Alana and laugh. "You're joking right?"

Alana pouts her lips, scrunches her nose and her eyebrows knit close together, as she tilts her head and stares at me. "No, why?"

I hand my books to Adriana who stands beside me, "Alana if you think that you can trust him, then you're even dumber than I thought." Alana looks at me in confusion.

"Alana, if he did this with me unknowingly and I go to the same school as you, who knows who else he is going to do this with."

"He says he loves me and he won't do it ever again."

"Oh, honey." I place my hand on Alana's shoulder and hold in my laughter. "Good luck with that."

FALL FOR YOU

FALL FOR YOU

"Some stories don't have a clear beginning, middle and end. Life is about not knowing, having to change, taking the moment and making the best of it, without knowing what's going to happen next.
-Gilda Radner

The tri-tone alert sound blares through the speaker of my iPhone. I turn the sound off on my phone and shove it in my back pocket.

I need to get out of here. It's almost 9:30PM and I told Mia that I would be done by now.

'Mia: Text Message' flashes on my screen. "Feli, when are you coming? He's here. We are all waiting for you."

"Almost done. I am leaving work in 5. I will be at your house in 15." I type rapidly and stuff my phone back into my pocket before my manager walks backs into the cash office. I finish preparing my deposit for the night and ensure the cash office is tidy.

Five minutes later, my manager checks my bags and jacket to ensure I didn't smuggle any product out the store with me. *Stupid rules. I'm not going to steal anything from Sport Chek.*

Once my purse and jacket are checked, I rush out the door and I speed home to get changed. I then speed to Mia's house where Mia, her boyfriend Anthony and his friend Matt wait for me.

Matt and I met at a club a few months back. It was the same day Mia met Anthony. Matt was supposed to come back to the hotel after the club, but instead he left and went to another club. Mia knows I think he's hot and she also wants me to date one of Anthony's friends, so Anthony and her set this whole thing up.

"Hey, I am down the street from your house. Tell your mom to hold your dog or else I am not coming in." I warn Mia.

When I arrive at Mia's house, I run out of my car toward the front door. Mia's mom opens the door as she tames the obnoxious, barking dog.

I hate that dog. He bit me twice! Every time I go to their house I make sure the thing is hidden before he attacks me again.

Mia's dog barks excessively as I rush up the patio steps. I miss a step, trip over my foot, and my knee bangs against the edge of the stone steps, as I collapse.

"Oh my God! Are you okay?" Mia's mom stares at me lying

on top of the steps. I attempt to hold back my tears.

I rest my hands and slowly peel my body off of the stone steps. I limp up the steps holding onto my knee.

"Ow," I wine and laugh at myself.

"Hey guys," I say as I limp into the house.

"What happened?" Mia worries.

"Your stupid dog was barking at me and I got scared. I missed a step and fell up the stairs outside."

Matt, Anthony, Mia and I laugh.

I plop myself onto the couch and Matt sits beside me. "You know most people fall down the stairs, not up."

"Shh," I hold my knee and laugh in pain.

"Let me help you," Matt elevates my leg onto the ottoman and rolls up my pant leg over my knee.

"Ow, Ow, Ow."

"What the hell did you do," Matt looks at the blood gushing from my knee. "And how the hell did you manage not to rip your jeans?" He laughs.

"I have no clue man," I look at my knee as the pain intensifies.

"Feli, you're a disaster," Mia says and hands Matt disinfectant cloths and some gauze and then hands me a water bottle and some Advil.

"Guys, I think we're staying in tonight." I smile at Matt as he continues to nurse my knee.

"Are you going to be able to drive home?" Matt asks, "If you can't I'm sure we can help you with that."

"Ugh, I forgot I had to drive home. I guess I will see how I feel before I leave."

Mia pops some popcorn and prepares some chips.

She hands Matt and I a bowl and keeps a bowl for Anthony and herself.

"Okay guys, let's watch a movie then." Mia suggests, "How about Hangover?"

"Sure," we agree.

Matt lies down behind me and rests my head on his chest as my legs rests on the ottoman. Mia and Anthony cuddle on the couch across from Matt and I.

ACE

ACE

"A wise girl kisses but doesn't love, listens but doesn't believe and leaves before she is left."
-Marylin Monroe

I shuffle through the doors of KIA and jolt to the reception desk that faces the showroom.

"Hey," I greet the receptionist. "Seraphine, right?"

"Yea, hey" Seraphine whines. As she sits in her office chair, her neck and head crunches down in her back and her long hair waves down over her back rolls.

"Is there anything you need me to do?" I ask. I am covering reception for the next few months here while one of the receptionists is on sick leave.

"No, just record the receipts and stock out these cars," she explains. "I did these ones already" Seraphine points to a pile of yellow and purple files stacked on the desk.

"Here is a schedule of everyone working." She scans the room. "This is Ace." Seraphine points to a tall man who hovers over the reception desk.

He wears a clean black suit and white shirt matched with a

skinny black tie. I stare up at Ace, "Hi." I smile. "I'm Felicia."

"Hello Felecia" Ace repeats my name in his soft Middle Eastern accent. "My name is Aseem." Aseem is from Afghanistan, so instead of people constantly mispronouncing his name, he calls himself Ace.

"So what do you want me to call you," I ask "Ace or Aseem?"

"Whatever you want," he smiles.

I don't know if he is being creepy or flirty. He's cute, but I can't seem to determine his age. His muscular body build tells me he's 28 but then his short vague sentences and the roughness of his face tells me he is 35.

After my shift ends, I call my friend Isabella on my drive home, "Bell?"

"Hel-lo, what's up?" Isabella replies as her Italian accent peeps through.

"Okay, so you know how I am covering at KIA" Isabella works for the same auto group who owns KIA. She works as a full-time receptionist at a location in Bolton.

"Yes?"

"So, there is this guy at the dealership I'm covering and he's kind of cute." I pause.

"Really?" Her voice amplifies, "was he flirting?"

"Ya, a bit. I guess. I'm not sure to be honest. But there is one thing."

"What?" Her voice clutches.

"He's kind of, sort of..." I pause and giggle, "It's not like I'm going to marry the guy."

"Feli! He's what?" Isabella demands.

"Um, he's Afghani."

"That's okay," Isabella replies. "Just don't get hurt and please be careful." She explains.

"I know I will. I am telling you he's just nice to have fun and talk to. I'm defiantely not getting into a relationship." I giggle.

"Good." Isabella sighs.

Scattered papers cover the reception desk. I gather them and position them into one big pile. Five minutes to close and there are no customers in the dealership. I shut off the TV, clean the coffee machine, switch the phone to night mode, and check my text messages on my phone.

Aseem: Meet me at the Tim Horton near highway.

"Okay, bye I am leaving now," I announce, then walk out the front door of the showroom and rush to my car.

I check my reflection in the rearview mirror. My eyeliner still outlines my hazel eyes. I touch up my bronzer and slap on a new layer of natural pink lip-gloss.

Now I can go. I take a deep breath and drive two minutes north of the dealership, where I meet Ace at a Tim Horton's facing a ghetto gas station in one direction and one of our chain dealerships in the other.

My old manager works at the dealership it faces.

I hope he doesn't see us.

"Hey," I smile and quickly close the passenger door as I get into Aseem's car.

"Hello," he says. He grabs my face and kisses me. "I wanted to do that so bad."

I blush, "Really? Why?"

"Because." His accent thickens, "you look so good."

It gets stronger when his voice pitches. His voice pitches when is excited or he is trying to pay a compliment or when he is explaining something. It's a bit of a turn off to me. But that suit. That suit. I mean, it's perfectly tailored to his body. No wonder he gets around.

"Oh stop." I lean back against the passenger window and evaluate Ace's attire for the day. Aseem is wearing a charcoal suit, lilac purple shirt, but no tie today.

Perfection.

Aseem drives to Lowes, just like every other day when we meet up after work. We go to Lowes parking lot and we talk about going places but we end up hanging out in the car all night. All he wants to do is stay in the car. He has only taken me to dinner one time. One time we planned to go to the movies, but we stayed in the car.

The only date we've ever been on, Aseem took me on a nice walk near the Lakeshore where we talked and embraced the beautiful view of the city. Aseem showed me an apartment building where he used to live, he showed me an area he hung out with all of his friends, and then he brought me to a dive restaurant where they sell Pho. It's some type of Asian soup that's made with beef stock and has thin noodles inside with little pieces of chicken or beef in it. Before this night, I've never heard of Pho. Aseem ordered some complicated stuff I and I ordered a plain chicken and noodle soup. It was good, but I was scared I was going to find a rat tail in my soup.

Lately, Aseem's been stressed because he hasn't sold any cars and now he's in charge of 'training' the new sales girl, Cassandra. I'm stressed because Aseem is 'training' the new sales girl.

The first day I walked into this place he hit on me. He also hooked up with the chick from service. He said they ended stuff because 'he changed'. What if he tries to hit on the new girl? They have been spending a lot of time together. I know his game. I am not stupid; I know when he is attracted to someone.

I text Aseem

Felicia: Are we meeting up after?

Aseem: Yes, Lowes.

Felicia: K

After work, Aseem races into the parking lot and parks beside my car. I have been waiting for fifteen minutes. He signals for me to come into his car.

"What the hell took you so long?" I slam the door shut as I get in.

"I was with clients."

"Did they buy?"

"No, I was helping Cassandra."

"Seriously? Like, you need to sell cars for yourself not other people."

"Felecia," Aseem breathes deeply. "I can't have you watching me with Cassandra while I am working."

"What? Watching you?" My hand reaches out and grips on top of the glove box, my other hand on the seat. "You think I am watching you? Aseem, I have a shit ton of work to do with licensing and stocking in fifteen cars. I have more important things to do than watch you."

I was watching him. Not in a stalker way. In a 'I'm jealous that your up the new girls ass' kind of way. Training. Smoke break. Sit and stare outside break. Client meetings. She's his new tail.

Rumors have been spreading that Cassandra and Aseem have been hooking up. The same rumors that were spreading when I started here and we hadn't even gone out yet.

"I saw you watching when I went for a smoke break," he admits.

"Aseem," I pause and take a moment to stop myself from ripping his head off. "I don't appreciate that you spend every fucking waking moment with this girl. Do you like her?"

"No, why would you even ask me that?"

"Maybe because the same thing that you are doing with her, is what you did with me when I started. I am not stupid. I do go to university, you know."

Aseem bites his bottom lip and holds his closed fist toward his mouth, "I don't like her. I like you. But you are not my mother, you are not my wife, and you are not my girlfriend."

"Um, excuse me did I say I was?" My back is pressed against the window. My fingers reach for the handle behind me.

"My point is, I don't have to report to you. I don't report to my mom. Why would I have to report to you?" Aseem looks sincere.

I hold my hand out, "I am going to stop you now. I never said you were any of those things, but I think I deserve the respect of you not doing that shit, especially in front of my face. "

"I'm sorry. I am just frustrated." Aseem rubs my leg for forgiveness.

I pull the handle and open the door, "Well maybe you should think about who you take your shit out on." I slam the door shut and storm to my car.

Asshole.

"I haven't spoken to him since I left yesterday at six!" I explain to my friends, Jessica and Vanessa, and their mom, Cathy. "Like it is now eight o'clock Sunday night and I haven't heard a word."

"Ew, this guy sounds like a complete loser." Jessica looks disgusted, "cut him loose Feli."

"Feli, she's right," Cathy pipes up from cutting up fruit in the kitchen, "You have to get rid of him."

Vanessa and Jessica nod in agreement. My phone rings. It's him. I stand up from the couch, look at my phone, inhale a large breath of air, and breath out.

"Hello," I answer.

"Hi." Aseem responds as if he had just woken up. "How are you?"

"Are you kidding?"

"What?" His clears up.

"You're seriously asking me how I am doing? You didn't even have the decency to call me last night or at all today."

"I was busy," he claims.

"Well, I am busy now."

"I don't want you to be mad," he begs, "I told you how I felt."

"Well you know what Aseem, I don't appreciate you saying that you report to me. If I ask you what you are doing I am asking you 'what's up' not 'hey did you just make a right at the lights?'"

"Okay," Aseem says "I just don't like having to tell you what I am doing all the time."

"Aseem, I don't care what you're doing all the time. Like you said, we're nothing so that it. There is clearly a language barrier and you're not understanding what I am saying."

Constant 'Okay's' and 'I'm sorry's' blurt out of Aseem's mouth.

He doesn't get it. He is set in his ways, like I am set in my ways, except my ways are right and his are wrong.

"This isn't working," Aseem says.

"You're right, it's not. You're not understanding what I am

saying. You think I am trying to control what you do, who you do it with and where you go."

"No, I just don't like telling you what I am doing all the time," Aseem explains.

"Listen," I bite my bottom lip "I don't care about every step you make. Yes, I call you and see what you're doing, as a casual conversation starter, which I tried to explain before."

I hang up the phone before Aseem can respond.

"That's it. I'm done." I plop myself on the couch, grab a handful of chips from the bowl beside me and shove it in my mouth.

SORRY, I DON'T FISH

SORRY, I DON'T FISH

"Because at the end of the day, all we can care about is looks! No one falls in love with your personality at first sight!"
-The Ugly Truth

B ut who are you texting on that phone?" I ask my friend Sarah as she gazes at her white iPhone.

"This guy," she replies and continues typing.

"Does he have a name? What does he look like?" Sarah ignores my questions as she tucks herself in the corner of the passenger seat in my car.

"Alright! I am going home if you're not going to answer," I giggle.

"Mark," a shock of light shines in my face. Sarah shows me a picture of Mark.

I rub my eyes from the brightness, grab the phone and examine the screen. A picture of a guy, who looks about 25 with dazzling blue eyes and coconut shell colored skin, appears on the screen.

"Holy shit Sarah, this guy is bomb, and how the hell did you meet him?"

"Don't say anything," she begs.

"Okay I won't," I clench onto my steering wheel. "Can you just friggin tell me man?"

Sarah sighs, "Okay, so I was with my friend and she was talking to this guy, and showed me a picture of him."

"This guy?" I interrupt.

"No, some other hot random guy. Anyways. She told me she met him on this site."

"No way! Tell me you joined a dating site!" I peak up from my seat.

"Ya, I wanted to try it out."

"What is it? Did you have to pay for it?"

"It's called, Fish In the Sea - otherwise known as FIS (pronounced fizz). Here look," Sarah gives me a tour of the site.

"Okay so this is my profile." Sarah shows me an organized screen, with a display picture of her in the top left corner posing at the mirror, and four small thumbnails of selfies underneath it. Beside her profile was her username, and then underneath was her biography.

"So like how many guys have you spoken to?" I plant my elbow on my glove box and rest my chin in my hand.

"A few, I am talking to a few now. There are a lot of creeps though." Sarah shows me different guys that she talks to. "Like I get about twenty messages a day, but maybe one or two out of the twenty guys aren't actually creepy."

"Really?" I giggle, "that's too funny."

"You should get one," Sarah suggests.

"Okay, make one for me." I begin looking through my Facebook profile, and through my camera roll for the best pictures of me. "Can you write my biography for me too, I am not good at that shit."

Sarah creates a profile for me.

"I'm a UFT student studying Professional Writing and Communication. I was born and raised by a nice Italian family, and my mom taught me what it is to be an independent woman. I admire Ellen DeGeneres and everything she stands for. I have a big personality and I am hoping to use these talents and have my own show one day."

I guess this will do. It's not wrong, I just feel like she made me sound like a Nonna, but maybe the whole 'nice Italian family' thing will score me brownie points, or in this case free bait.

Sarah adds the final edits to the 'About Me' section on my profile as I examine a selection of post-worthy selfies to add. The finalists include either, me smiling or repping the classic duck face pose. In every picture my hair looks beautiful, long and flowy. My face is brushed with the perfect amount of makeup that kind of has you guessing if I was wearing makeup, but there is no question based on the black bold eyeliner and mascara highlight my hypnotizing hazel eyes.

Buzz Buzz Buzz

Holy shit how do I turn these notifications off?

I have twenty messages from this app but I am only concerned about two, Chris and Daniel.

Chris and I have been chatting for a few days. He has a sarcastic personality – which I love because we joke all the time – and my eyes don't hurt when I look at him, well his pictures at least.

Yes!

I sigh in relief when Chris' message appears at the top of my screen after I open the app.

"You do hot yoga? That's hot. Maybe you can teach me one

day?"

Okay gross.

I scroll down to continue reading. "Does that mean you wear like yoga pants all the time?"

And, message deleted.

I see a message from Daniel further down the list.

Woohoo!

Daniel is more sensitive. I am kind of scared to joke with him because I am not sure how he will take it.

"Sorry, I fell asleep last night when we were talking."

Aw poor guy.

"Yea, well this weekend I am working late Friday and then I am spending it with my son."

He has a son?

"You have a son?" I reply immediately.

Daniel is nice and cute, but he hasn't sold me on going all Teen Mom now. I still need to figure out my needs let alone a child's. I am not ready to go all Step Mom on the kid so they can hate me and then we bond over a song and sing it in the house all night. Actually, that would be kind of cute. No Felicia, focus, no baby daddy's allowed.

Daniel replies, "yes, he is three and he is the best part of my life."

Doesn't every parent say that?

"Oh, well that's really sweet" I reply and delete the message.

I go through the rest of the twenty-eight messages that I received from last night. I want to see what the ugly fish said to me, some of them are funny others are just sad.

Carrot top Edward messaged me.

"Has anyone ever told you that you remind them of Picasso?"

What the hell? Picasso?

"A lot of people compare beauty to Mona Lisa, but not me.

I compare you to Picasso because when Picasso was doing his artwork he wanted to combine a variety of beautiful things into one perfect piece. Felicia you are a Picasso in my eyes."

Wow, smooth. Very smooth. I wonder how shit this guy really is?

I click on the thumbnail picture of Edward to view his profile and scan through his photos.

Fuck my life. Why do the nice ones have to be shit? I feel like I sound shallow, but isn't this what this site is about?

Edward says he 5'8, but on online dating that means like 5'6. It is obvious in his pictures with other people. They look as if they stand on stilts and then you drop your eyes down to find him. Edward says he has strawberry blonde hair and fair skin. It's orange and his skin is freckled. He does have nice blue eyes though.

I just can't.

I take a screen shot of the message he sent me, and a picture of Edward, and then go on to delete the message.

"Look," I send Sarah the screenshot of his message.

"Wow, that was so nice," she replies.

"I know but look," I send a picture of Edward.

"OH," she replies, "Well he has a nice personality."

If this girl tries and convinces me to continue talking to this guy she is crazy. She always says I am shallow but I am not. I just like being physically attracted to someone if I want to start anything with the person.

"I can tell he isn't your type so do what you want."

"I think I am going to delete the app, I am kind of sick of it." I reply, "They're all weirdos. The other day some 18 year-old kid told me that he is a king and he'll show me how to treat a queen."

"LMFAO" Sarah writes.

"I'm serious, LOL. I told him like sorry bud but I am not into younger guys. I let the kid down easy, but he still messages me and begs me to talk to him. Like get over it."

"OMG, I am dying right now," Sarah replies. "I had a few of those guys telling me how beautiful I am. I'm still talking to the guy from last week, he seems normal. I guess it's a hit and miss."

I laugh as I read my message from Sarah. "Well that's good. I'm still going to delete it for a bit and then I will see how I feel."

I press my finger on my phone screen and click the 'x' button on the corner of the FIS app.

A screen pops up, 'Are you sure you want to delete FIS.' I click yes.

I lie in my bed, curled up in the fetal position as if I am getting ready to leave the womb, and wrap myself in my duvet. I have my favorite Toronto Maple Leafs sweater on with a tank top and t-shirt underneath. Thick wool pajama pants are paired with my thick wool socks.

It's summer I shouldn't be this fucking cold. Ugh my head hurts. I just want to die.

My nose is clogged with green phlegm, my body feels like 100 degrees, but I am frozen.

I am bored. There is nothing to do when I am sick. I watched all my shows. I even watched the full series of 'Friends.' I grab my phone to update myself on Instagram, Facebook and Twitter. Boring, boring and more boring.

It's time.

I re-download the FIS app. After the download is complete and I sign into my account I check for any messages.

"I can see you being on TV one day." I read a message from a user Corellz90, "That smile is beautiful by the way."

Hmm, let's see this one.

I click on his thumbnail and look at his pictures on his profile.

Holy shit, he is actually hot.

Corellz90 has chocolate milk skin. His skin is brown but not too brown. It looks as if he got back from a vacation permanently. His eyes are small but they are so seductive, the way he squints when he poses for a picture. He looks like such a badass. He has a tattoo on his arm. I love tattoos.

Corellz90 has the hipster style going on. It's obvious in his selfies when he wears the beanie hat, paired with semi-fitted jeans and a classic V-neck t-shirt. The only thing he is missing is having blue eyes but his shaved head makes up for it, because I am sucker for shaved heads.

I hope he isn't a creep. I just can't be bothered to type back. I am too lazy.

"Hey, thanks." I reply.

"No problem, what are you up to?" He asks.

"Not much you?"

"Okay, listen I actually think you're cute and based on your profile you seem funny, so you have to give me more to work with." I giggle, and then I sneeze. "I just got in heading to my buddy's now."

"LOL I am sorry, I am literally super sick right now, which is why I am probably giving one word responses. Not intentional." I reply

"Aw, do I need to come make you pastina?"

I love him. Pastina is the best when you're sick. My Nonna made it for me all the time as a child even when I wasn't sick.

"I would love some pastina right about now." I reply.

85

Corells90's real name is Luke Cardola. He's Portuguese, Guyanese and Italian. His profile says he's 5'8.

I hope I am not as tall as him with my heals on.

"I think we found a winner" I text Sarah and attach a picture of Luke to the message.

FISHBOY

FISH BOY

"I know not everyone will like me, but this is who I am and so if you don't like it, tough!"
-Britney Spears

Thank God I don't work tonight, and I get off work from my internship early today. I usually work every Friday night, but tonight is my first date with Luke. Just two weeks after meeting on FIS, and I feel like I know him so well.

First, Luke and I would text each other so much, I had to start bringing my charger to work, and last week he started calling me. We talk on the phone for a minimum of two hours every single night.

We have a lot in common, and we figured out that he used to be best friends with one of my second cousins. Luke's parents are divorced. His mom is re-married with another kid and he has step siblings as well. The only difference is, his dad is also re-married and a successful businessman.

Tonight we are supposed to meet somewhere in Wood-bridge. It's halfway for both of us. He's in Thornhill and I am in Bolton.

I don't know what to wear. I want to look hot, but I don't want to look like I am trying to look hot. The other day I bought pale pink jeggings. Maybe I'll wear those with a white t-shirt and then a jean jacket to make it look causal.

What am I going to do when I see him? Do I hug him? Do I wait for him to hug me?

Luke is supposed to call me when he is done work. It's 4:00PM and I am on my way home from my internship.

The music in my car stops and my phone rings through the Bluetooth speaker.

"Hello" I answer in a high-pitched voice.

I must sound so annoying on the other end of this phone call.

"Hey, so I just go off work and I am going to go home and relax, shower and change." Luke says in his deep voice. When he talks it's like everything is just so mellow. No worries.

He seems too good to be true.

"Okay, so what time do you want to meet?"

"How about 8ish?" Luke suggests.

"Okay, that's fine. Just call me when you're leaving and we will decide where we are meeting after."

"Okay, I will talk to you later."

It's 6:45 and I'm already set to go on my date with Luke. While I wait for his call, I am going to stop by my friend Frank's house. He just bought a house and he's having people over tonight before the renters move in next week.

My friend Adriana, Frank's girlfriend, tells me to stop by at 7:00PM.

I apply the final touches to my freshly masked face of makeup. I smear my pink lip-gloss on my lips and brush a hint of bronzer to add a sun-kissed glow to my cheeks. I stare at myself in the mirror for ten minutes. There is not one flaw in my outfit.

I arrive at Frank's house and only a few of my friends are here. I sit in the kitchen with Adriana and Sophia, as Frank and Gianfranco – Sophia's boyfriend – barbecue burgers and hot dogs outside.

"Feli, you look bomb." Adriana spins me around to examine my outfit.

"Ugh, do I?" I fluff up my hair and reapply my lip gloss, "I don't want to go."

I feel my phone vibrate in my back pocket. It's Luke. He texts me saying he is running late and asks if we can meet around 9:00PM instead. The nerves in my stomach increase.

I may have to use their washroom.

"He said he has to meet at nine now," I announce to Adrianna, Sophia, and Isabella and Chloe – who just walked into the kitchen. They are the only ones who know about Luke.

"It's okay you can get your nerves out now," Isabella suggests.

We all giggle.

8:45PM more of my friends fill Frank's backyard. My cellphone vibrates in my hand, and my home screen flashes with Luke's name.

"Hello," I scream into the speaker. I can't hear anything. I walk away from the noise, and plug my ear.

"Hey," Luke says. "I'm going to leave now," he talks over the noise in the background.

"Okay, I'll call you when I am close."

I hang up the phone with Luke and stare at Sophia, and Adrianna, and Isabella and Chloe. They huddle around me wish me luck and send me off.

9:15PM I arrive in Woodbridge at a Tim Horton's Luke and I agreed to meet at.

Luke leans on the trunk of his black 2006 Mustang.

Boom. Boom.

My heart begins to pump faster and faster. As I put my car in park, Luke walks toward my door to greet me.

He's even hotter in person.

Luke wears a black V-neck and dark jeans with classic converse. His hair looks freshly cut, shorter on the sides with a mini comb over on the top. Luke has a hoop nose ring.

He is such a bad-ass.

I turn toward the passenger window, take a deep breath, turn to Luke, smile and get out of my car.

"Hey," I say as he approaches me.

"Hey," Luke hugs me. "Where do you want to go? Do you feel like ice cream?" He follows me to the passenger side of his car and opens the door for me.

"Sure, have you ever tried Menchies?" I suggest and I get into his car.

"No, what is it?"

"It's like this frozen yogurt place, where you make your own and choose your toppings."

"Yum! Sounds good, let's go there."

Luke walks around to the driver's side of the car, hops in and drives us to Menchies.

We arrive at Menchies. Luke comes around and opens my passenger door for me. I get out of the car and lead him into Menchies. Luke holds the door open for me and follows behind me.

"So do you know what to do?" I ask.

"No," Luke giggles with embarrassment, "you have to teach

me."

I show Luke the different flavors of ice cream you can choose from. Chocolate, Vanilla, Birthday Cake, Red Velvet, etc., and point to the little sample cups so he can see what flavors he likes.

I choose chocolate and cookie dough and birthday cake. After tasting every flavor, Luke chooses Red Velvet and Vanilla.

"Now, this is where the fun starts." I point to the counter of different toppings. "You choose what you want to mix in with your ice cream."

Luke goes for the fruit. I choose some Oreo bits and then strawberries and these little clear balls that when you eat them they pop in your mouth. I don't know what they're called but I get them every time.

After we weigh in our two ice creams, Luke takes out his wallet to pay.

"Thank you." I say as I grab our cups of frozen yogurt and find a place to sit.

I find us a small white table by the window. Luke and I chat and indulge in our creations.

The employees at Menchies are starting to clean up the yogurt stations. They mop the floor and begin stacking the chairs onto the table.

"I think they are closing," I say as I watch the employees clean up around us, the only two customers sitting inside.

"We can go in my car and talk then," Luke suggests. "I don't want to leave yet, do you?"

"No. Yea let's go in your car," I suggest.

Luke and I leave Menchies and head to his car. We sit in his car in the Menchies parking lot and continue to talk for hours. Luke loves to write. I love that Luke loves to write. He is very talented. I convinced him to read me one of his stories.

Luke pulls out a black notebook from his backseat and examines the pages. He chooses to tell me a story about a guy who visits his hometown. While driving through the town, he sees certain things, which trigger memories of specific love interests. Luke explains who each love interest was and how each symbol had a back-story to how he met her.

"This is a beautiful story," I stop him. "Like I can actually picture this happening as you tell me."

When he ends the story he lets the audience choose which path they want the guy to go on.

Luke blushes, "Well it's just an idea." He says.

"No, Luke I am serious you need to get this shit published and filmed."

Luke chuckles, "One day."

2:07AM

Luke drives me back to my car I left in the Tim Horton's parking lot.

"Well this was fun," Luke says. "I feel like we already knew each other. Like it wasn't awkward at all."

"I know. Okay well I am going to go."

Luke leans in to hug me. I hug Luke. I hear a kissing sound. *Was he trying to kiss my cheek? Was he going in for a kiss?*

"Okay bye." I rush out of the car and immediately into my own car parked next to his.

I pull out my phone and send a text to my friends.

'I just left.' Sent at 2:15 AM.

OLD
SCHOOL

OLD SCHOOL

"-Where to miss?
-To the stars."
-Titanic

I shuffle through the door and race down the stairs. All my friends fill the basement and welcome me as I enter the room. I search to find my phone buried under my wallet at the bottom of my purse. I check my phone for any messages. Bianca text me. She's at the front door. I text her back and tell her to walk in the house and come down to the basement.

Bianca walks down the stairs to the crowded basement where my friends and I socialize. "Okay guys, we're going to go to the movies now," I announce. I wave my hand goodbye. No one acknowledges me.

Okay cool.

I nod my head and walk up the stairs.

"Feli, hurry up we're going to be late for the movie!" Bianca shrieks. She pulls me toward my bedroom.

"Bi, I just got home from work you need to chill out." I throw my clothes off my messy bed and attempt to find my leggings.

"It takes like twenty minutes for previews anyway." I spot my black leggings popping out of my drawer and search my closet for a long sweater to pair with it.

Bianca nudges my hip and picks a sweater out for me. "I know," she says, "but the movie starts in like five minutes." Her eyes widen as she stares at the time. "Let's go!"

"What? Bianca, I wont be ready." I struggle to find socks, a clean pair of underwear and a brush. "Oh my God! We'll just have to go to the later one."

Bianca brushes my hair as I slide on a clean pair of underwear and then slips on my boots as I put on my sweater. We rush back downstairs to say bye to everyone.

My friend Dave sits at the back of the room on the shoulder of a couch. I hug everyone on the couch goodbye. Sophia, Gianfranco, Adriana, and Christian. "Bye" I say. I stop at Dave. He stares in the opposite direction of me toward the stairs. "Dave!" I slap his arm.

Dave jumps from my slap and stares at me "What!" He snarls.

"Aren't you going to say bye to me?" I twinkle my eyes, hold my arms out and smile.

Dave chuckles. His rosy cheeks turn a darker shade of red. He lifts up his muscular arms and pulls me in for a hug. I sneak in a sniff and sigh at the succulent cologne seeped into his skin.

He always smells amazing.

Bianca calls my name, but I continue to hug Dave. Her voice slowly disappears with the rest of the sound in the room.

Dave and I sneak upstairs, away from the crowd. I crawl up the stairs with Dave on my back. We hyperventilate with laughter.

"One more," I grunt. My hand hits the platform of the

stairs. "We made it!"

"Felicia I don't know why you had to hold me." He says.

"Because you didn't think I could." I smile, "and I have to prove you wrong."

"Yea okay bud," Dave cocks his eyebrows up, "that's never going to happen."

"Okay, whatever shut up," I giggle and punch him in the chest.

Dave and I sneak around the hall and find an empty room. He pulls me close to his tall, smooth, chizzled body. He holds me tight against his chest. We stand and gaze at each other and the room temperature rises. Our faces move closer toward each other, our lips barely touch. Dave sighs and looks down at my lips. I smile.

"What would your boyfriend say about this," Dave whispers.

"Boyfriend?" I slightly push back. "I don't have a boyfriend."

"Yea you do," He insists.

"Really? Well what's his name because I sure haven't met him," I throw my hands in the air, and then cross my arms and wait for a response.

"You think I didn't see you leaving Frank's house early the day when we were all there?" Dave uncrosses my arms and grabs my waist.

He's talking about Luke, the Fish Boy.

"I know you were going out with a guy that day, or else why would you leave?"

"Okay, relax over there." I laugh at Dave's assumption. "I didn't know you were a detective."

The night he is talking about was my first date with Luke.

"And that guy isn't my boyfriend." I confirm and rest my palms on his chest.

"What is he then?" He pulls me closer toward his body.

"A: It's none of your business and B: he is a random guy I went out with a few times. So you can calm your horses." I smile and tilt my head to look into Dave's eyes.

"I don't care, I am just saying, wouldn't he mind?" Dave looks down at me.

I nod in agreement holding in my chuckles. "Ya. I'm sure."

Our lips touch. I melt into his body as he pulls me in closer. He kisses my lips, he kisses my cheek, moves down, and kisses my neck. Thousands of tingles absorb my body. They move through my legs into my arms, into my chest and into my lips.

Beep beep beep.

The sound grows louder and louder. I can't feel Dave anymore. I search for my phone on my body. My eyes gently open.

Found it!

My phone beeps continuously with the annoying sound of my alarm tucked under my pillow.

I look down at the screen to shut off the infuriating beeps.

Fuck it's 10:00am I need to get up.

RECEIPT
BOY

RECEIPT BOY

"Your's are the sweetest eyes I've ever seen."
-Elton John

I slouch in my chair, my neck sinks into my back as I stare at the customer standing in front of my bank teller wicket. His clothes are painted in dirt, and his hair sticks out in different directions as if he just took off a hat.

"Hi," I smile.

"Hey," his perfect white teeth and ocean blue eyes smile back at me.

"Can you insert your card, please?"

He hands me a cheque to deposit into his account. I look down at the cheque, Benjamin Diaz. A box pops up on my screen 'Tell customer to remove card'.

"You can remove your card please." I turn my back to the customer to look at my supervisor Amanda sitting behind me.

"Um, Amanda?" I ask. She looks up at the customer in front of my wicket.

"Yeah, he's fine." She replies. I need her permission for any transactions over my limit of fifteen hundred dollars.

I proceed to deposit his cheque into his account. "Is that everything for today?" I ask.

"Yes," he mumbles.

"Okay would you like a receipt?"

"No thanks."

"Okay, thank you, have a great day."

"Thanks, you too," he walks toward the doors outside.

"Actually," Benjamin pauses. "Can I have twenty bucks?"

"Sure, can you insert your card again?"

Benjamin inserts his card and keys in his pin. I withdraw the money from his account and hand it to him.

"Okay, here you go twenty dollars," I say as I hand Benjamin the money. He reaches to grab the twenty-dollar bill, but grabs my hand instead. My head pops up, his head pops up. Our eyes meet and my heart plumps and my stomach rumbles. We stare at each other for a whole seven seconds. Fireworks explode around his messy hat hair.

"Uh, thanks," he clears his throat.

"Uh, yea you're welcome." I shake my head out of the daze.

Benjamin walks out the door and the bank is empty. I turn to Amanda. "Those eyes though."

"I know. He comes in every Friday," she says. "I think he had a thing with the girl Katrina who used to work here."

"Really? Well he's a cutie. Finally! There are never any hot guys that come in."

Amanda giggles. "Now you have some eye candy. Ya, he's probably one of the best looking guys that come in."

"For real," I agree. "But why does he feel the need to run out?"

"I don't know, he never wants his receipt," Amanda explains. "I always just say 'okay you can go' because there is no point for him to stay. It's just a deposit."

"True." I pucker my lips and nod my head. "Well his name is Receipt Boy." I say and stare into a daze of just Receipt Boy's blue eyes and me.

One month later.

The bank is silent. Amanda tells me how she has been with her boyfriend for six years, and he has yet to put a ring on it. Martin, the balancing teller, offers to talk to Amanda's boyfriend. Amanda, Martin and I giggle.

The door swings open. Receipt Boy drags his mudded Timberland work boots across the floor. Martin and I stand up straight.

If he serves him, I will kill him. He knows I want to serve him. It's the only time I can have a thirty-second conversation with him. I need to get my weekly fix.

"Hi there," Martin and I greet Receipt Boy.

"Hey," Receipt Boy walks toward me.

I knew it. He loves me.

My hands begin to sweat, my legs shake and butterflies absorb my stomach. "Can you insert your card please?"

Receipt Boy inserts his card and keys in his pin and hands me his paycheque. I stare down at the cheque. I check the date, and I check the name and proceed to deposit his cheque.

"Is that everything for today?" I ask.

"Yeah," he replies.

"Would you like your receipt?" I ask.

"Uh," he pauses. "Sure."

My eyes brighten when I hand him the printed receipt.

"Thanks," he smiles, turns around and walks toward the

door outside.

I wait for Receipt Boy to leave and turn to Amanda who's trying to hold in her laughter.

"Okay, Amanda that's progress." Amanda giggles, "He never asks for his receipt." I sink into my seat and gaze to the ceiling.

"It's true love," Amanda says. I giggle. "But you're right he never asks for his receipt."

"Maybe he thinks you're hot." Martin chimes in on the conversation.

"I have no problem with that."

"Just talk to him!" Martin yells at me.

Maybe he is annoyed with my Friday night report of my encounter with receipt boy.

"It's not that easy, I get too nervous," I explain. "Plus I don't know what to say."

"You're such a loser." Martin snarls.

"You do it for me," I say.

"Okay, I will" Martin is serious.

"No don't I'm only joking." I laugh.

After work Amanda, Martin and I head to Montana's - across the plaza from our work place -for some fajitas. It's our Friday night ritual to gossip on what drama is going on in the workplace.

"Felicia, just add him to Facebook," Martin blurts.

"No, I don't want to look like a damn creep," I say.

"Yea, man," Amanda adds. "You have to at least have a conversation with him that doesn't include asking him if he wants his receipt."

"Do you want me to add him?" Martin asks.

"Do whatever you want."

Martin searches Receipt Boy on Facebook, by his real name, Benjamin Diaz. Within two minutes Receipt Boy accepts the request.

"Oh my God! Martin, you actually added him?" Amanda covers her face. I grab Martin's phone out of his hand and look through Receipt Boy's profile.

"Now he is going to think you're gay and you like him," I suggest. Amanda and Martin giggle.

Two weeks later.

"Thank you have an excellent day," I say to the old woman who hunches away from my bank teller wicket.

I organize my work area and announce, "I can help who's next!" I look up at the line of customers and see Receipt Boy standing in front of me.

"Hey," Receipt Boy smiles and inserts his card into the debit machine.

I look over to my co-worker Nina – she works in the day-time– and she smirks at me.

"Hi, how are you?"

Inhale. Exhale. I learned it in Yoga. It keeps me calm when I am nervous and stressed.

"Good," he replies and hands me the cheque.

"Soo.." I look at the cheque and verify all the appropriate information is there. "You're off work early today." I blurt out.

Oh my gosh, did that sound creepy?

Receipt Boy's head pops up. He smiles, "Yeah actually I have a dentist appointment so I got off early." He explains, "Actually, it's even better because I just found out I don't have to work this weekend."

Okay, he's going with it. Now keep going, just don't fuck it up.

"That's good. Wait, this weekend? You have to work on the weekends?" The pitch in my voice rises.

"No, no not for this job." He giggles, "I work as a VJ downtown at a club."

"Oh that makes sense. What club?" I ask

"Have you heard of Oak?" He asks. Oak overplays electric dance music. Ravers and drug use are rampant.

Ugh, I hope he's not into drugs.

"Yeah, you work there that's alright," I nod. "What's a VJ?" I ask.

"You know those screens behind the DJ booth with all the visuals showing?" Receipt Boy draws out an imaginary screen in the air and shows me where it is placed. I nod my head in agreement. "Okay well, those things you see on the screen is what I do."

"Oh so basically you trip people out." I say.

He laughs and agrees, "Pretty much".

"Okay, well is that everything for today?"

"Yeah,"

"Would you like you're receipt?"

"Sure," he smiles and I hand the receipt to him. "Bye, thanks."

"No problem. Have fun not working this weekend." I wave goodbye.

Receipt Boy walks out the doors. Nina looks at me in shock. "Oh my God I am so proud of you." She nudges me.

"I honestly, don't know what the fuck came over me. I just thought to myself 'fuck it just do it' and I did it." I wipe the sweat off my upper lip.

"Your conversation lasted forever though," Nina stresses. "I was thinking to myself 'look at this girl talking up a storm!' We need to tell Amanda when she gets back from lunch."

"She's going to be so proud." I jump up in my seat.

"Okay, so now, you need to keep having these conversations and see where it leads," Nina says.

"Well, now that he told me that he works at Oak, I can pretend that my friends and I want to go there for Halloween or something like that. I'll message him on Facebook and see if he can hook us up with tickets," I plan. "Then, after we fall in love, we'll add each other on Facebook."

"Oh yeah that's a good idea," Nina says. "You go girl. I can't wait to see what happens."

NICE-A-BOY

NICE-A-BOY

"Boys, if you like her, if she makes you happy, and if you feel like you know her, don't let her go."
-Nicholas Sparks

F eli!" My Nonna calls for me in her thick Italian accent. "Come-a downstairs and mangia la toast." My Nonna is staying at my house for about a week while my mom travels for work. It's great, my room is spotless at all times and the meals are always delicious.

I squint my eyes open and look at the bright screen of my iPhone that blinds my eyes. It's 9:00AM and I have to be at school for 11:00AM.

"Twenty minutes," I yell.

"Chi? Feli you gotta go a la scola," her voices gets louder as she walks up the stairs, down the hall and into my room.

"Nonna, please. I need twenty minutes." I shove my face into my pillow.

My Nonna opens my blinds and begins cleaning my room. The bright sun shines throw my window.

"Okay, fine" I peel myself off my bed, drag myself down the hall and gradually walk down the stairs toward the kitchen.

My Nonna has a plate of toast layered in butter waiting for me on the kitchen table.

"Feli, why you so-a-tired?" She follows me to the kitchen. "What time-a you sleep?"

"Three," I reply and stare down at the toast.

"Feli, you can no go to bed so late! Why you up so late?" Her voice screams in my ear.

It's too early.

She yells because she has trouble hearing, and because she's Italian.

"I was talking to a guy." I chew my toast and stare at the plate.

"Yea?" Her eyes pop out of her head. "You have a boy-friend?" The pitch of her voice increases with excitement.

Why did I mention I was talking to a guy? I know what she does when I say I have a boy that's a friend. Here come the questions.

I giggle, "No Nonna, he is just this guy from the bank. He's not my boyfriend."

"Why he no you boyfriend?"

"Because Nonna, we just started talking." My Nonna looks at me with uncertainty.

Oh no here comes the speech. The same speech I get when she thinks I am lying to her about not having a boyfriend.

"What do you mean? Is he a nice-a boy?"

"Yes," I nod and begin to laugh.
This is not helping you Felicia.

"Why you laugh? Is he you boy-a-friend?" She asks again. "Feli, if he's a nice-a boy and you like and he have a good job, and he no drink and he no smoke and he no do drugs, then you make him you boy-a-friend." My Nonna stares at me for a reaction and continues her speech before I can answer. "Then when you fall in love you come to my house and I make the pasta."

I take another bite of my toast, smile and nod.
She'll get over it.

I drag myself into my Monday morning class. My hair is thrown up in a messy bun and the bags under my eyes look like the black lines football players wear on their face.

"Are you okay?" Leila chuckles.

"Ya, I'm just exhausted." I sit in the chair next to her in the second row of desks. I rest my bag on top of the desk and use it as a pillow to support my head. "Shh." I lay my head on top of the bag.

"Okay, Boungiorno a tutti," Signora Apicella walks in and slams her book on the table that sits in front of the chalkboard.

My head lifts up. I wipe my eyes and attempt to listen to my professor talking about modern Italian cinema. The only problem is the movies she is discussing took place in the 1800's.

As my teacher faces her back to the class and writes on the chalkboard, I whisper to Leila. "Guess who I was talking to all night last night."

"Who?"

"Benji! We talked until 4AM. Poor guy had to get up for 5 AM."

"No way? That's great what did he say?"

"He's just amazing. He's perfect." I sigh.

"Okay that's great but what did he say?"

"Well it was his birthday yesterday so we talked more at night. Honestly Leila, he told me a lot of stuff, a lot of personal stuff. He said that he's never told anyone these things before."

"That's amazing," Leila says, "Just take it slow and see where it goes.

Friday.

I haven't seen Benji since last week, but we've been talking constantly since the weekend.

On Wednesday he told me he scored Raptor's tickets and he was bringing his friend. Then he told me he would've asked me but he 'already asked his friend'. I wasn't even fishing for an invite, but I took the opportunity to flirt and I told him he owed me. It got awkward becasue then he said, 'Oh maybe I shouldn't have asked.' I feel like he was joking. But what if he wasn't?

I know he likes to stay in and watch movies, so tonight I suggested that instead of a movie night, we could grab coffee. I messaged him at 3:00PM, it's now 7:00PM and I know he's seen the message.

Twenty minutes pass and the bank is silent. I can hear the noisy people who own the bakery next door, yelling outside. The door swings open. I look up. It's Benji. He walks in covered in mud with his phone in his hand.

"Hey," he lifts his head up to face me. His eyes shine through his tanned skin.

"Oh, hey." My body tenses and my hands shake as I deposit his cheque.

"How was your day?" He asks.

"Good, yours?"

"Ugh, I am exhausted. I worked a twelve-hour shift. I just want to go home and sleep." He whines.

"Oh really," I fake sympathize. "You're being a Debby downer." I print his receipt and hand it to him.

"I know. I just want this day to be over."

"Is that everything for today?" I smile.

"Yea, thank you." Benji waves goodbye and walks out the

door.

I turn to Amanda, who sits behind me. "Is that a joke?"

"Wow, I can't believe it. You better not message him."

"Oh, no I'm not."

Three hours later, Benji messages me. "Sorry for being a downer tonight."

Oh okay no problem now you can go suck an egg, thank you.

I wait twenty minutes to reply. I need time to think of what I want to say.

I text my friend Bianca for advice, and she suggests I tell him off completely.

Bianca doesn't really like Benji. I don't know why, she doesn't even know him. I guess he just rubs her the wrong way.

I reply, "It's fine. You probably could've used the coffee then."

He replies immediately, "Nope. I'm off coffee. All about green tea."

"Darn, I should have said tea then." I reply ten minutes later and Benji doesn't respond at all.

A few months have passed since that awkward conversation. Benji hasn't come into my work a lot because he works construction and there' s no work for in the winter, so he's forced to go on unemployment.

I love not seeing him, but when I do his eyes draw me in every time. I can't have that. He's nice, but he's rude. He shows interest but doesn't do anything about it. I don't even know if it's interest or him just being nice.

No guy is ever 'nice' to a girl, unless he wants something. I know form experience.

He does like to keep in contact with me. The other day he offered to help me edit stories for my courses, because he is a writer as well. I took the offer because I need all the help I can get.

But why all of the sudden, would he offer to help me?

I decide to finalize our situation by messaging him on Facebook. Benji's status is set to online on Facebook Chat. I open up a conversation with him and begin typing.

My fingers tremble and my heart beats faster as I type each letter. "Hey, I know this is random but I have a question."

"Sure, what's up?" Benji responds immediately.

I take a long, deep breath.

"You know I am grateful for you helping me with my stuff, but why did you randomly offer to help me? I'm just confused about that part."

"Well, you offered to help me, so I thought I would return the favor." He explains.

Yea, in like November when we first started talking, or whatever that was.

"Wow, not many people think like that, so thank you."

Just do it. Get it over with. You have nothing to loose at this point.

"I just don't get you." Enter. Message sent.

"I don't think there is anything to 'get'," Benji says.

I sit and lean back against my headboard of my bed.

I re-read his reply to myself three times.

"Yea, you're right. Forget I said anything." I reply, exit the conversation and continue working on my homework.

"Feli!" My Nonna calls my phone, "How's you friend?"

"Which one Nonna? I have ten," I joke.

She responds with her classic lecture, "No! One!" I picture her holding up her index finger in my face. "Feli, you supposed to only have a one boy-a-friend. If the boys see you have-a ten boy-a-friend, they no gonna want you."

I laugh, "I know Nonna. And that guy, he's a scemo."

"He no like you? Feli he just wanna sing and dance."

I hold the phone away from my ear and laugh hysterically. "Nonna."

"It's true. You find a nice boy-a-friend. You make-a-sure he smart like you and your mother. You beautiful Feli." She says.

"Thanks Nonna. Okay I am going to go and do homework bye love you."

"Okay, ciao Bella di Nanna. I lave a you too."

OH
SNAP

OH SNAP

"I am not a toy you can play with when you're bored or lonely or horny. I am not the girl the guy gets at the end of the movie. I am not a fantasy. If you want me, earn me. Until then, we are done.
-Scandal

My supervisor Amanda walks around the bank and ensures everything is locked up. I sit in the waiting area, pull out my phone and take a SnapChat selfie, and type 'work blows' as my caption.

I select specific people to send the selfie to.

I click on Mark, a guy who I made out with a few years ago when I went to Blue Mountain for the weekend with my friends.

I click on Dom, my friend from high school who I hooked up with two years ago. I thought I liked him, but really I was going through a mental breakdown realizing Nick had a new girlfriend.

I click on Dave, just because I know he secretly loves them even though he'll never admit it.

I click on Frank, Adriana's boyfriend just because he gets annoyed of my selfie SnapChats.

I click on Bianca, just because I know she is going to tease me about it later.

I click on Christian, a good friend from school. We have great SnapChat conversations. We sing to each other and send ugly selfies to one another or even just pictures of black, and reply to each other through short captions, instead of simply texting.

I click on Adriana, but I know she never opens them.

I click on Luke, just so he can see what he's missing.

I click on Justin, a random guy I met though Instagram who's super hot, but his last name is the same as my mom. His family is from the same town in Italy as mine. I feel like we are somehow related. I will only go as far as SnapChatting and maybe some flirty texts. I get grossed out and I have visions that our kids will have some kind of mental problems because there is that chance that we are actually cousins.

Dom replies to my SnapChat with a duck face selfie of him lying down and the caption "Hey cutie, miss you."

I leave the bank, and when I get into my car I call Bianca, "So Dom just SnapChatted me."

"Really?" She sounds excited, "What did he send?"

"Well, I sent the Snap of me I sent you and then he Snapped me back and said 'hey cutie miss you."

"Did you reply? Send him a hot selfie." She suggests.

Bianca's excited because she loves Dom and thinks he's cute and thinks I should date him, especially because he's single now. He was dating a girl but we all knew it wouldn't last. No offense to him.

"Ugh, fine hold on." I click on the SnapChat app and reply to Dom a duck face selfie with the caption "Miss you too."

"Did you send it?" Bianca yells through my speaker.

"Yea," my stomach is in knots. "He replied, he asked me to go for a coffee."

"Oh my God, go!" Bianca insists.

"Yea Bi, he probably just wants to get laid. But whatever I'll go."

Dom and I plan to meet at the local Starbucks for a coffee tonight. I had my grad photos taken today, so I am looking extra hot tonight.

"Hey Feli," Dom walks toward me and hugs me.

"Hey," I hug him back and walk inside Starbucks.

Dom insists on paying for my coffee. We sit in my car and catch up on life.

"How are you doing?" I ask Dom with sympathy.

"You know what Feli, what's done is done. I was obviously hurt, but I am better now. I am doing me and enjoying the single life. What about you? How are you doing?"

"Well," I explain, "I'm focusing on my school right now. I don't have time for guys to interrupt my life. I don't even know how I would make time for a boyfriend if I had one. I am literally either working, at school, or at home doing homework."

"That's good Feli, but no guys?"

"There is one guy but to be honest he's really weird."
I'm talking about Ben.

"Why what happened?"

"We talked for two weeks straight and it was amazing. The texting was mutual. He is so kind and I feel like I can share so much and be myself with him but one day I feel like he fell off the face off the earth."

"What do you mean? Did he get back with a girlfriend?"

"To be honest, I have no clue. One day he told me he had Raptor's tickets and then mentioned how he was going to ask me but asked his friend instead — I wasn't fishing for an invite, in fact I never even expected one — but I joked and said he had to make it up to me and after that it got all weird."

"That's really odd." Dom thinks of scenarios of why Ben would do that. "I don't know what happened there Feli, but don't worry because you're an amazing girl with a big heart and you'll find someone."

"Thanks Dom," I blush. "But I am not worrying about that until I am done school."

The car is silent. Dom stares at me. "Yea good for you." He continues to stare.

What is he staring at?

"You okay?" I joke.

"Yea, Feli I just want to say I asked you for coffee tonight because I want to make sure we're good."

Wow. He is talking about a few years ago when we had a 'thing'. I thought I liked him but he liked this girl, actually he was 'in love' with her. I told him before I never liked him. I thought I did, but he was just there and it was convenient, especially the night we went out for his birthday and I ran into Nick and his new girlfriend. That night, Dom and I hooked up and then the next day he texted me saying that it was a mistake.

"Dom, it's over. I am not going to lie, I did hate you for what you did. That was low, but I am over it now. I have moved on and as I said before, I never liked you. You were just there and it was convenient."

Dom looks disappointed, as if he wanted me to like him.

"Okay Feli, as long as we're good."

"To be honest, I thought you were here because you were 'bored' and wanted to 'have fun'."

Dom's eyebrows raise, and his mouth opens in shock, "Feli really? I can't believe you thought that, but I mean if you're down I am down."

I laugh.

I knew it.

"Yea, whatever we'll see how things go. I am not looking for anything serious though."

"Agreed," Dom lends out his hand for me to shake. I shake it. "Do you want to start now?" Dom shrugs his shoulder, and leans his head to the side.

"No can do, I need to go home and do homework. Also, I am not prepared."

Dom and I giggle.

We are in the midst of holiday get-togethers with Christmas coming close. My cousin Maddie is dragging me to Crabby Joe's tonight for drinks with her friends. Dom wants to chill later, so hopefully we don't stay here all night.

Liam, one of Maddie's obnoxious friends walks around the table and gives everyone a drunk motivational talk about how his life is great and he's living his life. He said that he's at his prime right now and that he loves the single life and didn't realize how much he was missing out on.

Liam stops at Maddie and I. "This girl," Liam's voice slurs and he points at Maddie, "she's a great girl you know." Liam gets really close in my personal space.

I lean back away from Liam, "Oh yea," I nod.

"Yea, like Maddie I need to find a girl like you. She's a girl you can't just have sex with her, get her pregnant and leave her. You have to stay with her, actually I wouldn't even do that to her." Liam explains.

I glance at Maddie. Maddie rolls her eyes and slaps on a fake smile.

"You'll find a good one Liam." I say.

"But you," he looks at me, "Like I can do that to you and like leave you and you won't care."

I feel my face turn as red as a little girl who peed her pants in front of the whole class.

"Liam," Maddie interrupts him.

"Um, what?" I ask.

"Feli, I am not saying it in a rude way. I am just saying you guys are different people."

"So, you're saying people can just knock me up and chuck me to the curb. So, if I ever get pregnant they don't have to even help me raise the kid?"

The expression on Liam's face turns from happy and jolly, to worried and scared.

"Feli, that's not what I am saying."

"Just go," Maddie pushes Liam away. "Don't listen to him that's not true." She consoles me.

My phone flashes. I have a text message from Dom. He wants to know when I will be done so we can hang out. I reply to Dom's message claiming I was busy and ask for a rain check.

I seclude myself from my friends, in the front of the bus limo, on our way home from the New Year's party and cry all the tears of my life onto the leather seat.

Tonight my friends and I celebrated New Year's Eve at a club Downtown Toronto. I've been sick for the past week and decided to drink away my sickness.

Tonight Dom was acting very weird. He treated me as if I was nonexistent. He ignored me the whole night. When the clock stroke midnight, Dom turned his head and completely ignored the fact that I was standing right beside him.

"Feli, why are you crying?" Christian tries to comfort me.

"Because," I sob into the seat and sniff in the snot that slips down my nose. "I am sick of people disrespecting me." I yell into the leather seat.

"What do you mean? Who disrespects you?" Christian rubs my back.

"People just take advantage of me," I say crying. "They only talk to me when they want something from me and I am sick of it!"

"Who does this to you though?"

"I don't know, everyone. Like what Liam said is true," tears continue to pour down my face washing away any makeup I had on.

Christian wasn't there, but I told him what Liam said the other day.

"What? Feli you know that's not true. People don't see you like that. You can't let shit that Liam says bother you. The guy is an idiot." I laugh and begin to wipe my tears. "Feli you need to think about yourself and what is right for you, not anyone else. You can't let what people say affect you."

I catch my breath from the hard tears, "Okay." I wipe my tears and lie on the seat for the rest of the ride home looking up at the lights on the ceiling of the limo.

"Just leave her," Christian advises the rest of my concerned and confused friends. "She'll be fine."

Dom has texted me for three weeks straight wanting to hang out, but I keep pretending I am busy. I tell him I have homework. I tell him I have plans. I tell him whatever I can to avoid seeing him.

Adriana calls me on her way home from work, "Did you go to Dom's the other night?" She asked.

No one knows about Dom and I, except my friend Bianca and my cousins.

"No what do you mean?" I ask Adriana.

"Oh well Frank told me Dom had everyone over on Friday because his parents were out of town," she explains.

Oh so I was good enough for him to text on Saturday to hang out because he had a free house, but he forgot to invite me when all my friends were at his house!

"Oh nope! I didn't get an invite."

"That's weird, I thought he would've asked you."

"Yea, me too." I hang up the phone with Adriana and text Dom.

"Dom we need to talk."

"Okay Feli, what's up?" Dom replies immediately.

He better be nervous.

"Listen, I just feel like this thing we have going on isn't working. I don't feel respected as a person by you. I feel like a piece of crap."

"What do you mean? Feli, I don't want you to feel like that."

"Okay that's sweet, but I do. I am just not comfortable with this, and I don't feel like you're treating me as a friend."

"Feli, listen I respect you as a friend. I love you and you are the sweetest girl I know with the biggest heart. I know on New Years I was acting kind of weird, I just didn't want people to know what was going on between us."

Yea, he didn't want that girl that he used to be in love with to know what was going on. Get over it.

"Well, thanks I appreciate that. I just want to be treated as a person and not an object."

"Feli, I completely understand and I want to make it up to you. If you want we can meet up now."

I wonder what he wants to do? Maybe he'll take me out for an 'I'm sorry' dinner. I don't know what else he can really do.

"For what?"

"What ever you want."

"Can't" I reply.

I close the conversation and ignore Dom's messages.

FLASHBACK

Flashback

"It was real, wasn't it? You and me. Such a long time ago, we were just a couple of kids. But we really loved each other didn't we?"
-The Notebook

I race to the pharmacy counter at the local drug store and hand in my prescription.

"It's going to be about fifteen minutes." A lady with long dark hair, nice plumped lips glossed in red, wearing a white smock stands behind the counter. "Are you going to wait or would you like to pick it up after?"

"No, it's okay I'll wait." The lady smiles, and hands me a buzzer that will notify me when my prescription is ready to be picked up.

I browse the store for something to buy. My friend Christina walks in with her mom.

"Hey how are you?" I approach Christina.

"Hey good, I heard your joining Anytime Fitness here, in Bolton, Adriana told me."

"Yea, I am doing that special offer they have for ninety days. We're going on vacation and I need a workout buddy to keep

135

me motivated."

"Yea, it's better than —"

Oh fuck, I look like a disaster. Does this really have to happen to me right now? Like what am I wearing? These baggy leggings make me look like I have a penis and I have pimples all over my face.

"Hey," I stand up straight and look behind Christina to see Nick walk in. A girl wearing a bright pink sweater follows him.

It's probably his girlfriend. Just say 'Hi' and then continue your conversation.

"Hey, how are you?" Nick's mom Daniela asks. She pauses and waits for my response.

Way to make it worse. I haven't seen Nick and his mom at the same time since we've broken up. I have seen them both on separate occasions, but never together.

"Hey, oh my God! I'm good how are you?"

I really want to chat with her. I have to skedaddle out of this conversation.

"Good, just picking up a few things."

"Yea, me too. Well it was great seeing you." I say.

He looks so hot. Like why is it that he looks good and I look like ass? Way to show him what he is missing Felicia.

A look of disappointment masks Daniela's face.

"Wow, that's awkward." Christina says as Nick and his mom roam the aisles. "This is what happens when you live in Bolton, you run into everyone."

" I know," I wrap my arm around my stomach, turn my head, stare at the aisle behind me and look for Daniela. "Okay, anyways I will message you when I go to Anytime and maybe we can go together?"

"Sure," Christina says and proceeds to the cash register with her mom.

I walk to the prescription counter and ask if my prescription is ready. My buzzer didn't go off yet, but I need to get out of here. My prescription's still not ready. I roam the nail polish aisle and the makeup aisle and the shampoo aisle and the toothpaste aisle and the card aisle. Nothing is helping this feeling in my stomach.

Should I talk to her? I haven't seen her in over a year. Last time I saw her she told me I should go by the house. I told her I wouldn't because Nick has a new girlfriend and that would just be extremely awkward.

I walk down the shampoo aisle again and see Daniela examining a Pantene Pro-V conditioner bottle. She looks up at me, her eyes brighten.

"How have you been? What are you up to? Are you still in school?" She grabs my arm with excitement.

Nick walks around the corner and stands behind Daniela. Nick smiles and winks at me.

You're making it worse when you wink at me you know that right? I thought I was over this whole thing. It has been way too long. Maybe the feelings are just distracted by my nerves. Yea that's what it is, nerves.

"Good," I grab the bottom of my hair and begin stroking it. "Yes, I am still in school it's my last semester, thank God. What about you guys? How have you been?"

"Oh my goodness, that is amazing. I am so proud of you. You know, graduating from university is a great accomplishment. Not many people can do it."

I blush. My eyes wander to Nick. "Thank you. Yes I know trust me I have had my fair share of mental breakdowns, but I'm happy it's almost over. I just need to find a job now."

I think she wants to hug me. She grabbed my arm when she was congratulating me on my 'success'.

"How is your mom? I talked to her a couple years ago I think. Maybe less."

Nick looks at me. Memories flood my brain.

Daniela called my mom for advice on her mortgage. My mom works for a company where she manages financial companies, who hand out mortgages to people. My mom helped her about seven years ago, when Nick and I first began dating. Last time I ran into Daniela she asked me for my mom's number because she needed to talk to her. One day Nick came into my work and I asked him about that phone call our moms had – even though I knew how it went – and he responded very short. I know what's going on. He knew that I knew.

I look at Nick, "I feel like it was around last May. And my mom is good you know, the usual."

I wonder what he is thinking. I wonder what he feels. He probably doesn't feel anything. I shouldn't be feeling anything. I was doing so well. This sucks.

"Well tell her I say hi. How old is your brother now?"

"Um, he's turning ten in April."

"Wow!" Nick says as he walks toward the cash register.

"Wow eh, time flies." Daniela says.

"Yea how old is Adam now?" Adam is her youngest son that she had with Nick's step-dad.

"Seven. He is having his communion this year."

"Wow, no way. He's so big now, I remember when he was first born."

Sympathy fills Daniela's eyes. I can tell she doesn't want to leave. "Well it was great seeing you I have to go paint the bathroom now. Tell everyone I say hi."

"It was great seeing you too, and I will." I wave goodbye.

Buzz. My prescription is ready.

ABOUT THE AUTHOR

Felicia Paulozza was born in North York in 1991, and grew up in Bolton, Ontario. Felicia graduated with a degree in Professional Writing and Communication, and Women and Gender Studies from The University of Toronto in 2014.

When Felicia is not studying or writing, her hobbies include singing in her car, taking selfies, spending time with friends and family and always finding a way to entertain everyone around her.

"Be yourself, everyone else is taken."
-Oscar Wilde

Don't forget to check out my blog at

www.shortgirlandhighstandards.com

Made in the USA
Lexington, KY
07 June 2014